Stirrings of the Soul

Evangelicals and the New Spirituality

Michael Raiter

MATTHIAS MEDIA

Stirrings of the Soul
© Matthias Media, 2003

Matthias Media
(St Matthias Press Ltd. ACN 067 558 365)
PO Box 225
Kingsford NSW 2032 Australia
Telephone: (02) 9663 1478; international: +61-2-9663-1478
Facsimile: (02) 9663 3265; international: +61-2-9663-3265
Email: info@matthiasmedia.com.au
Internet: www.matthiasmedia.com.au

Distributed in the United Kingdom by:
The Good Book Company
Telephone: 0845-225-0880
Facsimile: 0845-225-0990
Email: admin@thegoodbook.co.uk
Internet: www.thegoodbook.co.uk

Distributed in South Africa by:
Christian Book Discounters
Telephone: (021) 685 3663
Email: peter@christianbooks.co.za

ISBN 1 876326 62 X

Cover design and typesetting by Joy Lankshear Design Pty Ltd.
Printed in Australia.

To Sarah

With love and gratitude.
Some people write about true spirituality,
you daily model it before me and others.

Contents

Giving credit
where it's due

IN LATE 2000, Dr Paul Barnett, then Bishop of North Sydney, invited me to participate in a series of lectures to be held in his region of the Anglican Diocese of Sydney, entitled *2001: A Faith Odyssey*. Paul asked me to address the topic of 'The Spiritualities and God's Spirit'.

Little did I realise, at the time, that I was about to open a Pandora's box of spiritualities. And what a collection of spiritualities! New Age, feminist, environmental, evangelical, occult, mystical, animal, vegetable and mineral ... now I'm getting carried away! Books have been written on any *one* of these spiritualities, and I was being asked to survey the whole field.

Mind you, I could hardly have been asked to comment on a more important topic. The explosion of interest in spirituality in our society, and I suspect in Western societies generally, is nothing short of phenomenal. If you advertise a public address on religion or Christianity you will be hard pressed to muster up much interest from a disinterested and cynical public. However, if your theme is 'spirituality' then you are far more likely to draw a crowd. Very few people today would not willingly admit that they see themselves as spiritual beings, and such people are open to explore and experience some of the many and various spiritualities that are readily available.

As I began to investigate some of these spiritualities it soon became clear that, diverse as they are, they also share a great deal in common. I suppose, in that sense, they are like people themselves. You hear two apparently conflicting comments about people. On the one hand, we're told that no two people are alike. We're all like snowflakes, each with his or her own unique character and design. Yet, we're also told that people are basically the same, again like the proverbial snowflake. Despite the considerable cultural, ethnic, and linguistic differences between people, what we share in common as human beings, made in the image of God, is much greater and more profound, than what separates us. And, it must also be said, what we equally share as fallen creatures, "without God and without hope in the world", also transcends any other group or individual differences.

So with spirituality. While the characteristics of different spiritualities vary greatly, they all express common features. Contemporary spiritualities, while they may differ in their details, appear to be largely addressing the same questions. Further, the answers that they give to many of the most important questions of life and the remedies they offer also bear striking similarities to each other. Increasingly, spirituality as a topic, and as a part of people's self-identity, has moved in from the margins of life and society, to a place near the centre. The spirituality phenomenon is now such an important feature of our cultural landscape that it can no longer be ignored. It demands to be taken seriously. It demands some analysis.

This book is not designed to be a comprehensive survey of even the major spiritualities on offer in our society. That would require a far longer work, and would demand a depth of study and level of expertise that, quite frankly, is beyond me.

Besides, should someone want to read further on, let's say, New Age spirituality, there are already a number of very fine books written on this topic by experts in the field. What I hope will be useful, though, is a broader survey of the topic of spirituality. 'You can't see the forest for the trees', is often heard. Well, here we'll look at the forest. We won't be walking around the forest and examining each and every kind of tree in depth. Rather, we'll be standing on a nearby hilltop and surveying the forest as a whole. Certainly, we will notice that each kind of tree has its own distinctive features, but at the same time it can't help but escape our attention that all trees, as trees, share a great deal in common.

Further, as well as drawing upon a good deal of very fine work that has been done in the North American context, I will also try to examine the roots of the current spirituality phenomenon here in Australia. Of course, I am not breaking new ground in doing this, but it is important that we write in and for our own unique situation. Australia is not America, and in a brief and preliminary way, I want to help Australian Christians in their own encounter with this remarkable phenomenon. We will try to examine what the appeal of contemporary spirituality is for Australian evangelical Christians, and examine some of the issues that it raises for our own understanding of the Christian life. At the same time, these issues remain relevant for most of the developed, Western world in its post-Christian grasping for spirituality.

As I delivered my lecture at the 2001: A Faith Odyssey lectures series, and answered questions from the floor, it became very clear that most people were far more interested in satisfying their own spiritual thirst, than learning about the spiritual desires of others. What I heard from the floor, in question after question, is what I subsequently read in book after book on evangelical spirituality. And that is, that there must be something more in living the Christian life. Many Christians who love the Lord Jesus Christ and long to please him, seem frustrated that their spiritual lives are too often dry and lacking in vitality. Church services too often leave people flat and empty. They walk away bored, as emotionally, relationally and intellectually unsatisfied as when they arrived. And some walk away, and don't come back. To be quite honest, I felt some sympathy for their questions. Too often, over the years, I've visited a church and wondered, why do people come here? They must be indwelt by the Spirit of God, because there's no earthly reason why you'd endure a service like this week after week!

When you're thirsty you may be tempted to try anything which you've been told is tasty and refreshing. And there are plenty of alternatives, even on the shelves of the Christian supermarket. I knew then that I had to address the question that was being posed that night: is evangelicalism selling people short? Is there, after all, something 'more'? This is all tied up with the greater question, what is true spirituality? If we were to meet truly 'spiritual' people, what would they look like? It is these sorts of questions that this little book will try to begin to address.

I want to thank Paul Barnett for his invitation to address that conference, and for the course of study and reflection that it has led me to subsequently pursue. I want to thank the council of Moore College for kindly granting me six months study leave, which made possible the writing of this book. My sister, Ruth, put in countless hours of typing after a local thief, presumably a seeker after spirituality (!), broke into my house and absconded with my computer. Tony Payne and Kirsten Birkett from Matthias Media are two of the most perceptive editors a writer could hope for. Their advice has been invaluable. And, thanks especially to Peter O'Brien, Tim Bowden, and Andrew Cameron for casting wise, critical, but gracious eyes over the text. If the book's a bomb, it's comforting to know I can pass the buck!

Chapter 1

The Spirituality Explosion

A walk around the Mind Body Spirit Festival

Twice every year, for four days, Sydney hosts its annual smorgasbord of the spiritual and the supernatural, the other-worldly and the inner life, the mysterious, the mystical and the magical. Clairvoyants, consultants, soul channelers, and curers of the human spirit, compete to win your mind and soul (and, let it be said, your dollar as well), while they offer you physical, spiritual, social, economic and sexual wellbeing. It is the Mind Body Spirit Festival.

The centrepiece of the festival is the exhibition centre where over 200 different booths play host to a fascinating array of New Age philosophies, natural health cures, and traditional remedies. You can learn to relax with some aromatherapy or transformational breathing. You can open your mind—and, presumably your mouth—to holistic dentistry. Or, you can unlock your full potential with a few whiffs of fragrant bush flower essences. There are booths offering innocuous health appliances, like the 'Pure Magic' water distiller, and the 'Green Life' juicer. Or you can purchase an easy-to-attach support for back pain, whose "sturdy straps draw reverse pressure from your knees to keep your pelvis stabilized" (only $57, or $107 for two!). Or you can take a brochure for a bathhouse where you can escape the stress of city living, cleanse the body of those yucky unwanted toxins, relax the mind, and "emerge feeling wonderfully refreshed and rejuvenated" (for just $49 for 15 minutes).

However, by far the bulk of the displays offer therapies and healings which are far from innocuous, and introduce you to the multivaried world of modern spirituality. You can dabble in some tarot card reading or numerology. Or you can take a fast track to success by enrolling in neuro-linguistic programming. You can find lights to direct you along life's path by connecting with angels and spirit guides. The more adventurous among you can take a journey to another dimension in search of knowledge with Astral Travel. Or you can just explore the mysterious and esoteric truths of capoeira, ear candling, iridology, and auyurveda (making sure that you carry with you a not-so-concise Oxford dictionary!).

Like the food hall of a large department store, the exhibition hall caters for a variety of shoppers. There is the spiritual nibbler. This casual inquirer is someone who just wants to sample some of the physical and spiritual foods on offer. Such a person may not be a committed customer and is attracted there by simple curiosity. On the other hand, there are the more serious shoppers. These are the sort of people who are aware of that large empty space in the living room of their lives and are looking for just the right piece to fill that vacuum and give their spiritual home the balance and ambience it is crying out for. For these more serious inquirers the festival also offers a range of seminars and workshops.

I've paid my $13 admission fee. I've grabbed my show bag (courtesy of Nature Care College) and now join me on a stroll around these seminars and meet some of the festival's more colourful characters.

There's Madi Nolan, whose impressive credentials include the fact that she has cured wandering spirits in an Indian burial ground and brought new life to failed businesses. She offers Black Hat Feng Shui Cures for her clients who will develop the skills to "capture the images of earth ley lines, vortex centres and nature spirits". Part of the secret of her success is that she has a "powerful magic altar cloth from a monastery in Nepal". The customer is advised that if they bring a camera to her workshop, wear something red, and have their photo taken with the altar cloth, then 'spirit guides' often appear in the photos. The cures that will flow from learning these skills can change your life and health, and increase your income. The latter is particularly important, as this workshop will cost you $33 a ticket!

Or, if your love life has been a bit flat lately, you can learn from Oceana and Icarus. For just $66 a ticket you can get tips on Tantric lovemaking and relationships, and learn how to reconcile your sexuality and spirituality. They promote themselves as the world's foremost Tantra teaching married couple "who met at sunrise at the top of a mountain in the Himalayas". I can only assume they must have been wearing more on the top of that Himalayan mountain than they're wearing on their promotional brochure!

I am now beginning to watch my dwindling wallet more carefully. Still it's hard to resist an expert on the human soul, its origin in the universe, and its history on this planet. That's Ruthe Rendely, who has channelled angelic energies since 1995 when a high angel approached her to bring out the Seraphim Blueprint, an angelic system that was developed for the benefit of humanity in Atlantean times. Ruthe will also tell me how I can establish an abiding connection with one of the highest angels in the universe, the archangel Michael. I will learn that while this angel is often depicted as a warrior, his deeper essence is profound love and pure being, and that I can experience direct transmissions from him which will bring me into an experience of unconditional love and God-consciousness.

Then there's the workshop of Kerrie Edwards-Ticehurst where, using creative visualizations, meditation, chakras, clairvoyancy and clairaudience, you can learn to speed up your vibrations, so making it easier to make contact with the other side. Then through palm reading, jewellery reading, and interpretation of your aura you can "travel to your temple to meet your guides and then journey into past lives with these friends".

Finally, you can be tempted and charmed by Deborah Gray who, the advertisement tells me, is Australia's number one seller of books on white witchcraft. She followed up her successful first book, *How to Turn Your Ex-Boyfriend into a Toad* with *How to be a Real Witch*. Her workshop will teach you the basics of spell casting and sorcery.

The Mind Body Spirit Festival, however, is much more than a kind of New Age supermarket. Indeed, to brand it 'New Age' is not really accurate. Few today would own the expression. Of itself, it is confusing and ambiguous. Most people at the festival prefer to describe the advice and experiences which they offer as spiritual therapies. Clearly, these practitioners are offering different paths to enlightenment, but each with the same ultimate goal in mind: the attainment of wellbeing. Jesus said that "those who are well have no need of a physician, but those who are sick" (Matthew 9:12), and what all these folk are offering is holistic health and well-being to fractured, sick and frustrated people.

To people who are aware of the brokenness of their lives, or have experienced disappointments in their relationships, or are terrified by their own mortality, the therapies offered by the mind, body and spirit practitioners hold an undeniable appeal. Just listen to how some of these advocates promote their products. The neuro-linguistic programming (NLP) workshops claim they will help you "increase your income, enjoy better relationships, improve your health and fitness, increase your

competitive edge and profitability, communicate more effec-
tively, achieve all your goals, and give you a fast track to
success". Clairvoyancy and hypnotherapy will lead to
emotional fulfilment. Discovering the healing power of sound
will enhance your relationships with the self and others, as
well as giving you "energy, creativity and joy". Ayurvedic daily
rituals will result in optimal relationships, fitness and health.
Body-psychotherapy will enable your relationship with your
partner to become "truly intimate, passionate and happy".
Discovering more about the colours of your aura will "change
your life, empower your decisions and assist the healing process".

The focus is clearly on the here and now. Success in this
world. Wellbeing for the present. Yet, at the same time virtually all these therapies present themselves as being fundamentally 'spiritual'. That is, there is a recognition that if we are
going to realise our true potential as human beings and find
wholeness in our lives, then we are going to have to be willing
to accept that there are realities to human existence which
transcend the physical and material.

Devotees believe that the secrets to unlocking the meaning of
life or, more importantly for most people, the power to live a
holistically healthy life, are not found, ultimately, in the test tube
of a scientific laboratory. Neither will they be unravelled by
sending more space probes into the far reaches of the cosmos.
It is the conviction of the festival that there is another dimension
to people and the world which can be explored and experienced.
This is what is consistently promoted as 'the spiritual'. As
human beings form spiritual connections, then natural bonds
are re-formed which then can release people to experience their
full physical, spiritual, intellectual and social potential.

Some people make these connections through channelling

into the rhythms of life, and the sounds and colours of the world, all of which can be explored. For others, the path to wholeness is through making contact with the worlds of supernatural beings: angels, witches, and nature spirits such as elves, fairies and gnomes. Then others direct us to the wisdom of ancient sages from long forgotten cultures, or guides and masters who, having investigated and discovered spiritual truths, can today lead us along the same paths of self-discovery. For some, "the truth is out there". For others, the truth lies within. Yet all would agree that this truth, this power, this deeper reality, is both available and, having been connected with, carries the potential for the profound personal transformation of every part of a person's life and being.

In the free programme to the Mind Body Spirit Festival, the Founder/Director offers his welcome to all this year's visitors. He summarizes the overall theme of the festival as "natural wellbeing". The shopper will find little here that one could term familiar or traditional. The therapies on offer are deliberately alternative. He is confident that somewhere in the myriad of therapies each person will find "something that is right for you at this time". Welcome to the warehouse of wellbeing. Taste and see. Mix and match. Browse or believe. The salespeople are eager to win your custom. This is twenty-first century spirituality. Marketplace mysticism. And it is very, very popular.

A surf around the net

Time magazine on December 16th, 1996 ran an article entitled 'Finding God on the Web'. It began with the story of a community of monks who live and worship in a sanctuary deep into the desert of New Mexico. They live a simple lifestyle, twenty miles from the nearest power line, twice as far from the nearest phone, and an hour from anything that resembles civilization. In order to reach these monks, one follows the simple hand carved wooden sign which invites, 'Ring this bell'. There is, though, one other way to communicate with this remote group of Benedictines: e-mail! Using electricity from a dozen solar panels and a data link through a cellular phone, these monks have developed their own website, and can be contacted on porter@christdesert.org. Indeed, so successful have these monks proven to be that they have now developed a business designing and maintaining other people's websites.

Over the past ten years religious groups have rushed to go online. Indeed, the number of sites dedicated to religion and spirituality have grown at an astonishing rate. If you search on the internet for 'spirituality', you are presented with a myriad of sites, including one simply called GOD.com. GOD.com proudly announces that spirituality is the biggest thing on the world wide web. In a world hungry for experience and satisfaction, religion is more popular than sex. It boasts that if one asks the internet search engine Alta Vista to locate sites related to 'Sex' it will return 683,643 documents. But, request 'God' and it lists nearly three times as many: 1,772,945. So, the internet which is often portrayed as the domain of sin and sleaze is even more the home of the supernatural and the spiritual.

The variety and ingenuity of the new websites is staggering. The *Time* article reports that Mormon sites offer links to vast genealogical databases. 'YaaleVe'Yavo', an Orthodox Jewish site, forwards e-mailed prayers to Jerusalem, where they are affixed to the Wailing Wall. There are two websites devoted to a tiny, obscure Vietnamese group called 'Cao Daiism', a sect which worships the French novelist, Victor Hugo. Even the techno-phobic Amish people of Pennsylvania now find themselves unwittingly on the web, thanks to Ohio State University. This site, among other things, offers guidelines for installing a rear warning light on a horse-drawn carriage!

Not surprisingly, an increasing number of churches and parachurch organizations have jumped onto the internet bandwagon. If the adage used to be 'publish or perish', it is now 'online or outdated'. More and more churches have their own websites, both to keep their members in touch with church programmes and policy changes, but also in the hope of catching the attention of a web surfer, who may just happen to grab the wave of St Hildebrands in Netville, and enjoy the possibility of a surf in her direction. So, what would one find if one were to surf the web waves crashing down on to Spirituality Beach?

Firstly, 'surfing' isn't really the operative word. Once again, the invitation is to 'shop'. What we find here is a busy, highly competitive marketplace of holistic wellbeing, with each hawker seeking to outsell and undercut his or her competitors with a product that is simpler, cheaper and more effective than any of its rivals. Let us join the spirituality shoppers in this superstore of cyberspace.

The first site that I log onto is 'Enlightenment 101' and there I meet Marilyn and Donald Schnell, who will help me to discover and explore the inner realm of love and higher consciousness which is available to everyone. It looks like I have struck the jackpot first time, and will need to shop no further! The Schnells (rather self-deprecatingly) see themselves as standing in the same spiritual traditions as other Grand Masters of spiritual self-understanding like Moses, Christ,

Buddha, and Mother Theresa. The wisdom they offer is both old and new. It is in a continuous line with the teachings of sages from ancient days, and in that sense what they offer is ancient truths. Yet at the same time, they discern that this is a new spiritual era, in which people have been reawakened to their need for enlightenment. The shopper is enticed by the prospect that he or she may be one of few who will discover this life-changing truth; it is "What 99% of the World's Population Doesn't Know". Where does one look to find this secret of spiritual power? One need only look inside, for all the sufferings of the human condition are a result of one's disconnectedness with the "Inner Power, the Sacred Inner Sanctum".

What benefits are to be obtained through membership to this exclusive club? Astonishingly, the Schnells can guarantee nothing less than "unprecedented happiness", and "greater health, prosperity and peace to the world". With Enlightenment 101 dreams do come true, whether they are of greater financial success, finding one's soulmate, or building one's dream home. And all of this for only a $49 per month membership fee (Visa and MasterCard accepted).

But, of course, we want to know, does it work? Well, there are testimonies from those who have paid their dues and tried it out. Susan Witt says that she and her husband have been improving daily since they began. Bruce Brincklow finds the course more meaningful than a church service (which may say more about the church he attends than the course!), and Evie Boss, having completed the course and learnt to follow her heart, has found a new and satisfying career in music. Indeed, so dynamic is Enlightenment 101 that the Schnells tell us, "many people say that just by holding one of these Inspirational Letters in their hands, they feel the powerful buzz of spiritual energy". My mind begins to spin at the possibilities of what might happen if I was to wear something red, and hold one of these letters in one hand and Madi Nolan's magic cloth in the other!!

With such a commendation, I wonder if I should look further, but having emerged from the Mind Body Spirit Festival a trifle cynical, I decide to keep on shopping. My next website is 'Divine Revelation'. Once again I am told that the truth is not out there, but in here! There is a "still, small voice of God within" which, when listened to, spiritually connects us and enables us to solve the everyday problems of life. Inside of me is the source of wisdom, healing, intelligence, inspiration, peace and happiness. Through this course I can experience higher states of consciousness and inner contact with my higher self.

I confess that, at this point, this is all beginning to sound a little familiar. But what can it promise to do for me? I am told that I will gain more self-confidence, enjoy life more, have greater peace of mind, clear away negative feelings, improve my personal relationships, have the power to change anything I do not like, and take command of my destiny. Does it work? Susan Silverman testifies that this course "has transformed my life on all levels", while Connie Huebner says, "no matter how much sleep I get, I have lots of energy. I feel much more full of vitality and energy and dynamism than ever before". And if you ask Jay Reynolds more crudely what is the cash value of the course, then he will tell you "I've almost doubled my income".

It is a little difficult to decide between these two courses, which sound like different brands of the same cereal. I will try one more. 'Spirituality-4-all: a Proven System of Spiritual

Healing' shows promise. What will this do for me? I am informed that it "has melted away AIDS, cancer, broken bones, broken hearts, depression, poverty, fear, hate, desperation, terminal illnesses etc". What is the power that will release this state of utopia? It is the power of Love. Where is this power? Again, it is found within. The author writes, "I realized that God, Love, was not far off somewhere, but right there in my heart. We all have access to Love (which is) the most powerful force in the universe and it is yours for the sharing in unlimited supply".

How can it be that a spiritual force which reportedly can heal broken bones overnight, has remained undiscovered and untapped for centuries? The answer is, that we are now on the verge of a new and historic moment of discovery of the power of love. I really do not have to ask if it works, but just to satisfy my quickly diminishing curiosity I, again, read the testimonies. One person lived with ceaseless torture for fifteen years, and having read this book on spiritual healing, the next night slept like a baby and awoke refreshed, with no traces of former complaints. Another bears witness to having been "lifted from sickness to health, from sorrow to peace, from lack to plenty, and the most beautiful of all, from darkness to light". What will it cost me to have this experience of heaven right here and now? Just $12.95, with a 100% guarantee. Paradise would be cheap at twice the price!

It is clear that while each product presents itself as offering unique and distinctive guidance and help, there is a remarkable sameness about the kind of spirituality which is being promoted on many websites. There are recurring themes. There is the notion that today is the day of salvation. Or, to put it in more theological terms, there is an eschatological dimension to these spiritualities. The masters and gurus perceive that this period of history is unique and climactic. Another website, 'joy2meu', which offers a 12-Step formula for Spiritual Integration, asserts that we have entered into what Native American prophecies call the 'Dawning of the Fifth World of Peace'.

Another theme that pervades most, although not all, contemporary spiritualities is that they direct inquirers to look within for their wellbeing. Again, 'joy2meu' asserts that "the Saviour does not exist outside of us. The Saviour exists within". Vivation is a method of spiritual enrichment, which allows spirit energy to enter every cell in the body. Advocates believe that we have parallel senses through which we perceive our inner world; we are internally visual, verbal, and emotional. By connecting with all this inner energy, then we can begin to discover health and happiness. Finally the benefits these programmes offer to their potential customers are uniformly extravagant and utopian. Heaven is available here and now.

Some of these websites are traditionally religious, some are atheistic, but all are spiritual. God appears with many names on the web. He is That Which is Greater, Higher Power, Truly All Powerful and Unconditionally Loving, Universal Force, Creator etc. His names and, indeed, his ontological essence may differ, but he is uniformly loving and supportive of his creation. He is not a God who comes accusing or judging. He is the God who banishes fear, and in its place offers and supplies the love and happiness which is the birthright of each of his creatures. For the medium of the twenty-first century, the internet, there is a god tailored to meet the likes and aspirations of the people of the third millennium.

A browse around the library

Let us make one more stop on our journey into the wonderful world of contemporary spirituality: the theological library. We are now in the realm of explicitly religious, and especially Christian, spirituality. Typing in 'spirituality' on the library computer, I am immediately greeted by ninety subjects which all, in one way or another, relate to spirituality. I can pursue spirituality and emptiness, or spirituality and emotion, spirituality and leadership, spirituality and liberation, spirituality and morality, spirituality and sexuality, spirituality and prayer, spirituality and remembering, spirituality and time, spirituality and work. I track down the spirituality sections of the library and wonder where to start amongst the almost 4000 titles that have been catalogued under the heading 'spirituality'. Let us sample a few.

Until recently, for most people the word 'spirituality' conjured up images of monkish-like practices of praying, fasting, and taking vows of silence. It was a term once associated largely with Catholic forms of religious devotion. Coming out of the contemporary Catholic tradition is *Soul Wilderness: A Desert Spirituality*. The author, Kerry Walters, tells me that, "To find God, we must go to the desert. Once there we discover that the desert, like God, is a great mystery".[1]

However, the desert is not just that physical wilderness, distant from the hustle and bustle of civilization, it is also a metaphor or an emblem of the inner life. This is the interior desert. In Christian monastic tradition the wilderness was the place where the soul had to journey if it wished to be purged of all its sinful accoutrements and find union with God. Similarly, the author argues that if we long for God to speak to our hearts then we must turn inward, into our individual inner desert and there remain until we break through into its secret. This kind of spirituality transcends and, ultimately, rejects reason; our inner desert is "a mysterious realm that stubbornly resists the battering ram of reason".[2]

While presenting itself as a form of spirituality consistent with a long line of Christian mystical tradition, it embraces the pluralism of the age. Walters draws upon insights from Zen Buddhism and his religious world view resonates with Buddhist themes. He writes, "If a person is ever to achieve enlightenment, she must first clear her mind and soul of all intellectual preconceptions about the nature of things".[3] In essence, desert spirituality is offering the seeker a profound relationship with the divine. Indeed, the final state in the abandonment of self is such a union with God that the soul becomes God. This is the true meaning of atonement, or at-one-ment; the great act "in which the nothingness of God-without unifies with the nothingness of God-within".[4] Desert spirituality presents itself as an invitation to the discerning reader, aware of his or her own spiritual alienation and isolation, to leave behind the safe, but tepid form of Christianity which has proven so unfulfilling and unsatisfying, and join this mentor on "the greatest human adventure": the quest for union with God.

If desert spirituality eschews the world and invites the reader to dive inside himself, *Asian Christian Spirituality*[5] is dismissive, almost scornful, of any spirituality which ultimately does not engage the individual with the realities of life. Here is a spirituality coming out of the ecumenical Christian stable. "Spiritual life", the book maintains, "is human life, the whole of human life inspired and led by the Spirit, the energizing presence and activity of God".[6]

The authors of this compendium of essays live and minister in Asia, in a world of many faiths and spiritualities. The authors discern the presence of the Spirit of God in all these faiths and, therefore, it is necessary to develop a spirituality that is universal and comprehensive. This spirit, which permeates all people, is the spirit of justice, freedom and struggle, and a spirituality that is appropriate for that context is seen to be one which is responsive to these existential realities. In short, then, spirituality is the response of the human soul to the diversity and condition of the world in which it lives. This reality is all-inclusive: sand, stone, earth, grass, trees, worms, birds, and humans in all the diverse cultural contexts. Samuel Rayan writes,

> The more open we are, the more spiritual, the more realities to which we are open, the greater the spirituality, the greater the depths and the profounder the meanings of reality to which we are open, the more authentic the spirituality.[7]

If 'spirituality' was once the domain of Roman Catholicism, and a term rarely heard from evangelical pulpits, or in discussions in evangelical home groups, this is no longer the case. Indeed, no one has taken hold of the rediscovery of spirituality with greater enthusiasm than evangelicals. *Satisfy your Soul: Restoring the Heart of Christian Spirituality; Streams of Living Water; The Soul's Quest for God: Satisfying the Hunger for Spiritual Communion with God; Subversive Spirituality; The Spiritual Quest; The Soul Search: A Spiritual Journey to Authentic Intimacy with God;* and *Authentic Spirituality* are just a few titles published in the last ten years by well-known evangelical authors.

Luder G. Whitlock's *The Spiritual Quest*, is typical of many of these books. Two premises appear to underlie the book. Firstly, there is a spiritual hunger and restlessness in the heart of many people, not least of all evangelical Christians, for deeper intimacy with God. Many Christians find the existing piety of their own churches or traditions stultifying, and long for a more experientially satisfying relationship with God through Christ. Whitlock, like others, begins his book with the famous words of St Augustine, "You have made us for yourself, and our heart is restless until it rests in you". For Whitlock, the answer, in part, is to recapture some of the lost 'disciplines of the Spirit', in particular, prayer and fasting. He notes that "these ancient spiritual disciplines, recently rediscovered by Protestants, may be of considerable benefit spiritually [as] they help people develop a focused emphasis on the inner life, on the all-important relationship with God".[8]

The second premise which drives Whitlock's book is that the current infatuation with spirituality by millions of non church-going people may well provide a critical 'window of opportunity' for the gospel. In almost unprecedented numbers, spiritual seekers are searching to connect with God and experience him personally. Whitlock observes that many of these seekers have been turned off by the church but are still open to a relationship with God that is authentic and meaningful. With the unbounded optimism that is such a feature of his American culture, Whitlock believes that this could herald an Awakening as great as the one which gave birth to the evangelical movement in the eighteenth century. Indeed, he believes that if Christians can seize this moment, then it may result in the twenty-first century proving to be the Christian century.

While other evangelical books do not reverberate with the same spirit of triumphalism that permeates *The Spiritual Quest*, nevertheless they all identify a spiritual malaise in the church. Very often, this dryness is something they, as writers, can testify to in their own lives. These books offer both counsel and practical guidelines to help parched souls find the spiritual sustenance and refreshment that they believe the Lord is longing to pour out upon them.

The sacred in Australia

This has been the briefest thumbnail sketch of, what is arguably, the greatest religious phenomenon in the Western world in this generation. While most of the contemporary analyses of the new spirituality are written from a North American perspective, there is evidence that spirituality is now well and truly part of the Australian landscape, as well.

When Sydney celebrated the new millennium with the most spectacular fireworks display in the city's history, it selected as its motto for the millennium the word 'Eternity', which was spectacularly lit up across the city's most famous structure, the Harbour Bridge. This word, in its readily identifiable cursive writing style, was made famous by the enigmatic reformed drunk, Arthur Stace. Stace wrote himself into the folklore of the city when, after his conversion, he spent the next twenty years of his life writing this one-word sermon across the walls and pavements of the city. In a city that is frequently touted as being one of the most secular in the world, which hosts and boasts the Gay and Lesbian Mardi Gras, one of the most popular events on the city's social calendar, it is striking that such a theme was both chosen, and warmly embraced by its population. While the word carried undeniable Christian resonances, for most people its appeal lay in the fact that it symbolized their awareness that there was something transcendent about the changing of the millennium.

Further, Aboriginal spirituality is now very much a part of the religious landscape of the country. The much-heralded Opening Ceremony of the 2000 Olympic Games included a presentation of features of traditional Aboriginal religious beliefs. Indeed, much of the Games was overtly religious: the sacred symbols of the Olympic movements, the flame and flag, the ancient Greek priestesses paying homage to the flame, the Olympic hymn and other sacred music. Once again, Australians enthusiastically embraced these religious allusions.

On my day of writing this opening chapter, the leading Sydney newspaper, *The Sydney Morning Herald*,[9] makes repeated references to the religious and spiritual life of Australia. The front page carries a less-than-sympathetic report of a public address by the Anglican Archbishop of Sydney, Peter Jensen, in which he called on Christians to take every opportunity to share their faith. The same front page introduces a five-part series on teenagers by profiling a 17-year old girl called Katrina who, we're told, is a practising member of the Greek Orthodox Church. Indeed, two-thirds of teenagers surveyed claim that they believe in a supreme being. Later in the newspaper, we will read of the work of two young Australians who are trying to teach motivational skills to teenagers. These young entrepreneurs are practitioners in neurolinguistic programming, timeline therapy, and hypnotherapy. The *Herald* also reports the visit to Australia of our most famous expatriate and feminist, Germaine Greer. A well-and-truly lapsed Catholic, Greer nevertheless argues for Aboriginal reconciliation because "we have to understand what sacredness is". She goes on to affirm that the land is "very holy", and that the nation ought to sign a treaty with Aboriginal peoples in order to "recover from our spiritual blight". The tone of the report conveys the paper's warm approval of the spirituality of Germaine Greer. In a nation where it is continually reported that formal religious affiliation continues to decline, there is an unembarrassed acknowledgement that we are people with spirits, and a nation with a soul.

As Christians, how are we to interpret this phenomenon, both on the wider front in society at large, and as it manifests and expresses itself in the church? Are we on the verge of a great spiritual awakening? While we may scoff at some of the more ludicrous and crassly marketed features of the new spirituality, does the movement testify to a deepening spiritual hunger in the hearts of men and women? If so, who is creating this hunger? Is it simply the natural and understandable response by a generation of baby boomers who, having swallowed the lie that "greed is good", and indulged themselves in unrestrained pursuits of material wealth and sensual pleasure, have now discovered that the consumer society which promised so much has, in the end, left them hollow and unfulfilled? Or are we seeing the promptings and urgings of the Spirit of God in these people? How truly spiritual is the new spirituality?

And what of evangelical spirituality? Have traditional churches presented people with an emasculated gospel, doctrinally pure, but stripped of all its relational and experiential dynamism? Or is this entire movement just another social phenomenon which the church blindly and unthinkingly has got caught up in? Rather than being spiritual leaders and prophetic spokespersons, are we once again part of a herd of spiritual thrill-seekers, bleating like the rest of society about the need to connect with the divine, and to experience his/her/its presence in our lives? These are some of the questions this little book will seek to address and answer.

Treatments of a topic like this usually attempt to be either sociological analyses, or biblical critiques, as if one cannot do both. In his examination of this phenomenon, evangelical psychologist Gary Collins asks how this new interest in nontraditional spirituality has become so popular. He argues, "The answer is not found in theology. Instead, the roots of the new spirituality are grounded in psychology and history".[10] Such a dichotomy is unwarranted. This new spirituality is profoundly theological, and scripture, even more so than history and psychology, informs us as to the ultimate origins and purposes of this movement. Any analysis of human society that is not refracted through the lens of scripture is both myopic and distorted. The word of God is God's timeless perspective on the human condition, and while it was written in, and to, particular historical contexts, its statements about the nature of men and women, and God's workings in his world, are universal and timeless.

Of course, we must also recognize that Christians live and minister in particular times and places and are subject to the same trends, movements, and events that order and mould the character of the society around them. To analyze evangelical spirituality, for example, in isolation from what is happening on the wider front with spirituality generally, would be as short-sighted as leaving the Bible out of the analysis. For all their insularity, Christians do not live in a bubble, and are as subject to the wider social trends as anyone else—although, hopefully, we are more discerning and critical.

In short, then, come with me on to a mountaintop from where we can see the entire landscape open before us. Hopefully, such a survey will help you to understand the spiritual character of the society in which God has placed you, and better equip you to speak the liberating gospel of the Lord Jesus to this society. But, also, from this vantage point, you may even better understand yourself, and your own spiritual yearnings and questions and, in the end, return with renewed confidence to the source of fresh water which is deeply and endlessly satisfying.

ENDNOTES

1   Kerry S Walters, *Soul Wilderness: A Desert Spirituality*, Paulist Press, New York, 2001, p. 1.

2   Walters, *Soul Wilderness*, p. 3.

3   Walters, *Soul Wilderness*, p. 4.

4   Walters, *Soul Wilderness*, p. 104.

5   Virginia Fabella *et al* (eds), *Asian Christian Spirituality: Reclaiming Traditions*, Orbis, Maryknoll, 1992.

6   Samuel Rayan, 'An Asian spirituality of liberation', in *Asian Christian Spirituality*, p. 20.

7   Rayan, 'An Asian Spirituality of Liberation', p. 22.

8   Luder G Whitlock Jr., *The Spiritual Quest: Pursuing Christian Maturity*, Baker, Grand Rapids, 2000, p. 23.

9   *The Sydney Morning Herald*, Monday 20th August, 2001.

10 Gary R Collins, *The Soul Search: A Spiritual Journey to Authentic Intimacy with God*, Thomas Nelson, Nashville, 1988.

Chapter 2

Defining the Indefinable

What is spirituality?

Much about the new spirituality must seem confusing to the casual observer. Not only is the variety of options overwhelming for this generation of 'spiritual seekers', even the terms people use seem elastic and imprecise. For example, when we see books entitled *Re-discovering the Sacred*, or *The Soul Search*, or *The Spiritual Quest*, do people mean the same thing by 'soul', 'spirit', and 'the sacred'? And when people outside the church use these terms, do they mean the same thing by them as evangelical Christians do? When Germaine Greer tells us that, "we have to understand what sacredness is", we would agree, but then wonder if anybody can really tell us what it is.

For many writers these terms are indefinable; indeed, to attempt to define them is to place constraints upon them which rob them of their power, their wonder, and their mystery. Phyllis Tickle in her book, *Re-discovering the Sacred*, writes that the sacred is something which can be perceived but never embraced. She argues that the sacred is to the material what perfume is to a flower; we know when we have ventured into its realm, but we are unable to articulate its essence. So, defining spirituality is like defining the fragrance of a rose, or the aroma of your favourite coffee. It is enticing and it is readily apparent when you are in its presence, but it is impossible to properly express what it is through the inadequate medium of words.

Further, Tickle affirms that the sacred is as essential to our being as our cardiovascular system is to our bodies, or the sun is to our world. She notes that we often associate the sacred with a place but, for her, it is not a place in a geographical sense, but it is "a place apart", a place where one experiences true aliveness, and feels properly at home.[1]

Thomas Moore's *Care of the Soul* was a very influential book in the 1990s, in which he maintained that, both individually and socially, the greatest malady of the twentieth century was "the loss of soul". Yet if one were to ask Moore precisely what this 'soul' is that we have forsaken, then he is much less precise. Indeed, he admits that a precise definition of the soul cannot be given. It has to do with genuineness and depth.[2] A leading North American analyst of contemporary spirituality, Wade Clark Roof, similarly recognizes that words like 'spirit' and 'spirituality' remain difficult to grasp. Nevertheless, he helpfully goes on to say that any adequate definition would include a reference to a relationship with something beyond oneself (God, or Other, or Transcendent Power). This relationship then brings meaning and value to life, and an awareness of one's 'inner self'.[3]

In the same vein, Australia's leading observer of the new spirituality, David Tacey, recognizes that "as time moves on, we find we are able to define spirituality less and less, because it includes more and more, becoming a veritable baggy monster containing a multitude of activities and expectations".[4]

Later on we will try to offer more precise biblical definitions of these terms, but for the moment we are examining how words like 'spiritual' and 'sacred' are used by contemporary seekers of the new spirituality.

Roof quite rightly recognizes that central to any understanding of modern spirituality is a quest for connectedness. Shannon Jung is a devotee of environmental spirituality. She recalls spending an hour in the Rocky Mountain National Park in Colorado watching a herd of Rocky Mountain sheep grazing on the mountainside. As she observed these beautiful creatures she wrote that she felt a "relatedness to the sheep". She went on to say that she had "to a degree become a part of their environment and they of mine". Then a bus of camera-clicking tourists roared up and scared them all away. But Jung was left with a profound sense of her connectedness to the natural world. She goes on to reflect, "I realized I was not separate from the sheep, the mountains, the meadow, rather I was part of the environment".[5]

This sense of being a part of the natural environment, and not just living in it, is seen as being profoundly spiritual. In a similar vein, one advocate of a feminist spirituality, Ursula King, recounts the testimony of one woman who, after a particularly traumatic experience in her life, recalls that,

> I woke up one morning, saying, I know where my loyalty and duty and love are owed: to my Mother, the Earth, who births us, feeds us, protects us, and takes us back into herself when we die, to give new life to other life forms.[6]

Once again, this woman's spiritual experience is deeply relational; she feels a sense of connectedness with the Earth.

This sense of a deep and potentially life-changing and life-enriching encounter with the Other is coming close to what people mean today when they speak of spirituality. Indeed, as the very word itself implies, it is an awareness of the aliveness of one's own spirit. This is a widely recognized phenomenon. Even the most sceptical analyst of the composition of the human being would affirm that people have a dimension or a part of themselves that transcends the physical. Whether we can rightly talk of people's constituent parts in this way will be examined later. However, at this point, suffice to say that in our society it is generally felt that the human spirit is seen to be something intangible yet essential. In the words of Wade Clark Roof, it is "that force which mysteriously and invisibly animates".[7] The exploration and experience of this spiritual dimension lies at the heart of contemporary spirituality.

At the same time, it is generally believed that a person's spirit does not really exist or function in isolation from the spirit which is seen to permeate all living things. Therefore, to be truly spiritual is to connect with this universal spirit.

When some Christians think of spirituality they think, naturally, of the ministry and activity of the Holy Spirit in the life of a person. But in contemporary spirituality the emphasis is anthropocentric more than theocentric. Modern spirituality is far more focused on the human spirit than the divine. One Catholic writer who studied Zen Buddhism found that it taught him not to search for a God on high, but "to look towards my inner being, facing my human nature".[8] Ursula King advocates, not praising God, but "self blessing" in which a woman affirms "the divine you".

If we were to ask advocates of contemporary spirituality, how it is that such spiritual awareness or illumination comes to birth in someone, then a common response would be that a person's soul becomes aware of its connectedness to all that is around it, both physical and metaphysical. Once one is aware of the transcendental nature of one's humanness then one begins a discovery of self-awareness, which then may lead to a growing understanding of the nature of the cosmos.

While a number of contemporary spiritualities recognize that only a few searchers have, as yet, discovered the particular spiritual secrets to success and wellbeing that they offer, all stress that such spiritual awareness and engagement is both normal and necessary. Whether the spirituality which is being spoken about is New Age, or aboriginal, or feminist, or evangelical, all writers on this theme affirm that questions about spirituality are the most fundamental in human life.

It will be obvious, then, that coming up with a definition of contemporary spirituality is no easy matter. And it would be difficult to find a form of words that would win universal agreement. However, let me offer the following as a definition of spirituality as the term is broadly used out there in the 'spiritual marketplace':

> *Spirituality in its broad contemporary usage expresses the longing of the human spirit for an experience of ultimate reality, through connecting to the spiritual realm, with a view to achieving inner contentment and a discovery of one's place in the wider cosmos.*

Of course, such a definition from a Christian point of view begs many questions. What is the human spirit? What do we mean by the longings of the spirit? What is this ultimate reality that, presumably, human beings are seeking for? These are questions that we will need to address as we seek to understand what the Bible has to say about spirituality and the contemporary 'stirrings of the soul'. For the moment, though, I hope that this definition will help you to understand what people mean today when they use the term 'spirituality'.

Religion and spirituality

Stephanie Dowrick, an Australian writer on 'the inner life', recently made the following observation about the distinction between spirituality and religion:

Spirituality was not a word I grew up with. Religion was part of most people's lives but it generally meant rules, dogma, received truths and tribal loyalties. There were certainly people within my orbit who were passionately devoted to their God. I am not sure, though, that even they would have spoken freely about a spiritual life or values. Nor would they necessarily have seen spirituality having a legitimate place outside organized religion. Yet it is probably partly because organized religion long ago ceased to meet the authentic spiritual yearnings of many people that "freelance spirituality" has gained such currency.[9]

Like many observers on contemporary spirituality, Dowrick is keen to draw a distinction between religion and spirituality. She recognizes, of course, that one may be religious in the traditional sense and still be spiritual; however the converse does not necessarily apply. A person can be deeply spiritual and not be a member of any organized or traditional religious group. Indeed, for many people their exploration of some aspect of "freelance spirituality" may be a very deliberate rejection of religion.

When you listen to practitioners of the new spirituality, you find again and again that they are making this same distinction between spirituality and religion. On the website entitled 'Spirituality-4-all', the writers offer inquirers 'A Proven System of Spiritual Healing'. One of them recounts their own discovery of Love, which is the first principle of spiritual healing. The person writes,

To me, the word 'God' brought to mind a set of creeds,

dogma, clergy etc. It was something for religious people, and I did not consider myself 'religious'.

This person would, nevertheless, consider himself or herself deeply spiritual. In his book, *Spiritual Marketplace*, Wade Clark Roof recalls a conversation with a 44-year-old woman who had grown up as a fundamentalist, Bible-believing Christian in North America. She had since moved to "a more friendly Christian Church". When asked about the difference between religion and spirituality, she had this to say:

Well, religion, I feel, is doctrine and tradition, genu-flecting, and you have to do things this way. Spirituality is an inner feeling, an allowance of however you perceive it in your world, in your mind, and however it feels is okay ... Spirituality, I think, is what enters you and lifts you up and moves you to be a better person, a more open person. I don't think religion does that. Religion tells you what to do and when to do it, when to kneel, when to stand up, all of that sort of stuff. Lots of rules.[10]

We have already observed that when many Christians use the term 'spirituality', they associate the word with those activities and behaviours prompted by the work of the Holy Spirit in their lives. Almost all of these people would, therefore, describe themselves as being deeply spiritual. Consequently, they may assume that when other people use this same term of their own yearnings and questings then they, of necessity, would also identify themselves as in some sense 'religious'.

However, as we have begun to see, much of contemporary spirituality vehemently denies that it is religious; at least in the

sense of having any association with one of the historic, traditional religions. And it is not just people who claim no formal
religious association who deny that their spirituality is religious; even people who happily identify themselves as
Christian, for example, are quick to qualify that this is not
something necessarily the same as being spiritual. In the
minds of such people, life is not about the search for religion;
it is a quest for the sacred. If that journey should lead one into
membership with a particular church or religious group, that's
fine, but that is only one of many valid and appropriate paths
to spiritual fulfilment.

Spirituality is spoken about as if it is the larger, primary,
foundational category of which religions are later, smaller and
secondary subsets. Speaking of the relationship between spirituality and religion, Episcopalian Phyllis Tickle writes,

> But the sacred is, of the two, the one that is common
> to all men and women, accessible to all humanity. And
> while no religion, I suspect, is possible for those who
> refuse to acknowledge and traverse the sacred, it is
> still true that religion itself is not essential to human
> existence. The sacred, on the other hand ... simply is.[11]

Tickle reflects what seems to be the prevailing view, that religion and spirituality are not, necessarily, the same thing.
Many, many people consider themselves spiritual, but only
some of them ever express this spirituality in forms that are
considered religious. Further, for many people, religion is a
perversion of spirituality, from which they had to be rescued in
order to truly discover and experience the sacred. Religion is
about crusty traditions, do's and don'ts, fear, shame, and
words, words, words. Spirituality is about liberating, subjec-

tive and soulful experiences.

Robert Wuthnow, in a survey of American attitudes towards religion, quotes one man who commented that religion, to him, means something like denominationalism, whereas spirituality is more the core of different religions. "Spirituality", he went on to say, "is closer to nature and closer to oneness with the planet".[12] For Stephanie Dowrick religion is all about difference; it divides people. There are Catholics and non-Catholics. Men and not-men. Whites and not-whites. Heterosexuals and not-heterosexuals. *Spirituality turns that around.*[13] What religion divides, spirituality unites. As people pray, enter the stillness, and leave behind their isolated sense of self, Dowrick observes that they then become aware of how interconnected their lives are. They then begin to understand the spiritual truth that she believes lies at the core of every religion: love and friendship.

In his discussions with many Australian young people on university campuses, David Tacey has observed that while most are rejecting traditional religions, they are very open to spirituality. He argues that it may not even be God they are rejecting, only God as he/she/it is presented to them in traditional formulations. He writes,

> Spirit is felt to be spontaneous, freely available and democratically structured, whereas religion is perceived to be doctrinal, regulated and authoritarian. Spirit is felt to be holistic and urging us towards wholeness and completion, whereas religion is perceived to be promoting perfection, one-sidedness and imbalance.[14]

As one reads discussions about religion and spirituality one can see the same themes emerging. It's perceived that religion tells you what to believe and what not to believe. It tells you what kind of behaviour marks you as part of the tribe, and what behaviours or attitudes render you an outcast. Consequently, religion robs people of their independence and their freedom to choose. At a time in human history when a world full of diversity needs to be brought together, it's being asserted that organized religion is often more a part of the problem than the cure. What, though, we all share in common as part of our essential humanity is that we are spiritual. Many advocates of the new spirituality are calling us to put aside the words that divide, and explore together the spirit that connects and unites.

Not only do many today disavow any religious affiliation, they are openly scornful of religion, and the Christian church in particular. In today's Western society, more and more people would claim that they are not religious or have 'no religion'. However, very few, even amongst the most secular, hedonistic, and worldly, would claim not to be spiritual. At the beginning of the third millennium it may be a cause of some embarrassment to describe yourself as 'Christian'. To be termed 'religious' still places you in the mainstream of society. But it is better yet to be 'spiritual'.

ENDNOTES

1   Phyllis A Tickle, *Re-discovering the Sacred: Spirituality in America*, Crossroad, New York, 1995, pp. 13-14.

2   Thomas Moore, *Care for the Soul: A Guide for Cultivating Depth and Sacredness in Everyday Life*, HarperCollins, New York, 1992.

3   Wade Clark Roof, *Spiritual Marketplace: Baby Boomers and the Remaking of American Religion*, Princeton University Press, Princeton, 1999, p. 35.

4   David Tacey, *The Spirituality Revolution*, HarperCollins, Sydney, 2003, p. 38.

5   Shannon Jung, *We are Home: A Spirituality of the Environment*, Paulist Press, New York, 1993, p. 2.

6   Ursula King, *Women and Spirituality: Voices of Protest and Promise*, Macmillan, London, 1989, p. 126.

7   Roof, *Spiritual Marketplace*, p. 34.

8   Yves Raguin, 'Deepening our understanding of spirituality', in J Arai & W Ariarajah (eds), *Spirituality in Interfaith Dialogue*, WCC Publications, Geneva, 1989, p. 83.

9   *The Sydney Morning Herald*, Saturday 14th July, 2001.

10 Roof, *Spiritual Marketplace*, p. 137.

11 Tickle, *Re-discovering the Sacred*, p. 13.

12 Robert Wuthnow, *After Heaven: Spirituality in America Since the 1950's*, University of California Press, Berkeley, 1998, p. 74.

13 Emphasis mine.

14 Tacey, *The Spirituality Revolution*, p. 31.

Chapter 3

The Rise of Contemporary Spirituality

WHY HAS THERE been such a 'spirituality explosion' during the closing decades of the twentieth-century, and into the twenty-first? How do we explain the fact that so many people today are expressing a fascination with, and indeed are actively participating in, different kinds of spirituality?

By the 1990s the fast-growing interest in religion and spirituality was no longer deniable. Religious themes permeated popular films like *The Matrix* and *The Truman Show*. Angels kept appearing on celluloid, disguised respectively as John Travolta in *Michael*, Nicholas Cage in *City of Angels*, and Denzel Washington in *The Preacher's Wife*. We even had *Angels in the Outfield*. Angels, witches and demons have also appeared in popular television programmes like *Charmed*, *Buffy the Vampire Slayer* and *Touched by an Angel*. But eclipsing them all was the phenomenally successful weekly exploration into the world of the supernatural and the paranormal, *The X Files*.

In book sales we also see evidence of the enormous community interest in spirituality. (It has been rightly pointed out that people in a poll might describe themselves as religious or spiritual, even if they don't actually put this confession into practice, but if they walk into a bookstore and spend $25 on a book then they truly have made a statement about what is important to them.) Analysts of the American scene record that in 1994, the country's largest book wholesaler, Ingram's, enjoyed a 249% growth in the area of religious books, and consequently decided to expand its inventory in that department. In the same year, the Association of American publishers reported that sales of books in the Bible/religion/spirituality category were up 59% nationally over sales in 1992. A Gallup study projected that in the twenty-first century the largest sales increase in non-fiction books would be in religion/spirituality (82% growth by 2010 over 1987). While sales in Australian bookstores would have been much more modest, even a cursory browse around a bookstore demonstrates the popularity of books in the New Age/spirituality/self-help categories.

This is all the more surprising given the well-documented decrease in religious affiliation of people born since World War II, especially in Australia. Weekly church attendance in mainstream Christian churches in Australia declined from 32% of the population in 1936, to 20% in 1976. The baby boomer generation has been tagged as irreverent and irreligious, and yet these are the very people who are riding the wave of the renewed interest in spirituality. What has led to this increasing cynicism towards more orthodox religion, in particular Christian denominations, and yet an attraction to less traditional forms of spirituality?

Spiritual alternatives

Clearly, the present infatuation with the spiritual can be partly attributed to the fact that many people for the first time are being exposed to more alternatives in the world of spiritual experiences. For example, the current political debate in Australia about reconciliation has led to a greater awareness of aboriginal culture and, as a consequence, aboriginal spirituality. That which was once despised is now both recognized and honoured.

Further, the world is a smaller place: a global village. In the seventies cheap air travel arrived in Australia. Overseas trips, which were a once-in-a-lifetime dream for most people, were now affordable and commonplace. South America, Asia, and Africa are exotic and attractive holiday destinations, and in such places people are exposed to a variety of religious beliefs and traditions.

Australia's commitment to multiculturalism has seen a large increase of immigrants from Asia and the Middle East in the last twenty-five years. The *National Agenda for a Multicultural Australia* enshrines in government policy the right of all Australians to practise and propagate their religious beliefs. People, therefore, are exposed to a variety of spiritualities that hitherto were only the province of a well-travelled few. Many of these spiritualities express an innate connectedness with the natural order. Whereas Christianity has traditionally emphasized mankind's dominion over the world, other religions emphasize our spiritual union with this creation. As a consequence, increasing global concerns over the future of our neglected, abused, and damaged environment have sensitized people to those spiritualities which express this kinship humans feel that they have with the natural world.

The role of the media

Few forces have been so influential in both promoting the new spirituality, and in moulding people's appetites for it, than the commercial media. Television, and now the internet, are replacing the traditional formulators and channelers of moral and religious values—the church, the family, and the school. The media not only expose people to the variety of spiritual options but, as Wade Clark Roof points out, they have a levelling effect on religious truth claims. He writes,

Belief in Hell, the wrath of God, and sin are de-empha-
sized; even 'religion' itself is often played down as a
humanly created thing in favour of 'spirituality', or a
God-thing as a frame of reference. The discourses in
which religious themes find a home tend to be highly
psychological: terms like *experience, fulfilment, happiness,* and *inner peace* all reflect a preoccupation with
the self as the dominant motif. Casting religion in
subjective terms meshes well with a highly individual-
istic, inward-looking culture, and particularly its
emphasis upon spiritual openness and expansion.[1]

Traditionally, moral and religious values have been passed on,
in part, via the society's stories and narratives. In today's
Western world, film and television are the storytellers, and
they define for us good and evil, right and wrong, truth and
promise. What is more, they promote the pluralism which is
so favoured by this generation. When you log onto the web,
you can choose between Anglicanism and Animism,
Wesleyanism or Witchcraft. Popes and pagans become equals
in the cyberspace staging of religious possibilities.[2]

Why is it that today's generation of spiritual seekers are
hungry for what the new spirituality seems to offer? Why,
indeed, do so many people refer to this generation as 'spiritual
seekers'? Why aren't we 'spiritual contents' or 'spiritual
malcontents'? What has given birth to this generation's fascination with spirituality, in whatever form it takes?

The seismic sixties

Mapping bygone social trends is a hazardous endeavour and it

must involve a good deal of speculation and subjective interpretation. However, hindsight does give one a perspective that
can be lacking when one is too close to the events that one is
describing and seeking to interpret. Social commentators of the
time described the 1970s as the decade that changed Australia.
The preceding decade was simply 'the swinging sixties'.
However, from the vantage point of the end of the millennium,
most social analysts now argue that the 1960s was the water-
shed period. Looking back it was even more 'the seismic sixties'
than 'the swinging sixties'.[3] It was the decade when, in the face
of cataclysmic political, economic and technological developments, traditional values were shaken and long-standing insti-
tutions like the family were changed irrevocably.

Those born into this period (that is, those born in the twenty
years after World War II) are referred to as baby boomers. In
many Western nations the period of economic prosperity that
followed the war saw a large increase in the number of
marriages and births. Today's Western leaders in business, poli-
tics, and education tend to be men and women born into this
baby boomer generation. They lived through a dramatic and
tumultuous period of social reorientation which permanently
changed and shaped their attitudes and behaviours.

In 1972, the Australian Labor party was finally returned to
office after more than twenty years in Opposition, riding on
the back of a famous election campaign, 'It's Time'. The time
for change had come. Certainly those dramatic three years of
Whitlam government saw significant and lasting social and
political changes. But social commentator Donald Horne was
right when he perceptively commented a few years later that it
was not those Whitlam years, but the seven preceding ones
(1966-72) that were the time of critical change. Those years

saw the dominant values of Australian society shaken and challenged—the same values that were being shaken throughout the Western world.[4]

The particular difficulty facing an Australian analyst of the effect of social change on people's religious values, is that most of the material available is written about the American situation. Australia is not America, despite their shared colonial roots in Britain. The cultures are significantly different, and this difference is no more obvious than in attitudes towards religion. Stuart Piggin has colourfully contrasted the modern origins of these two British colonies: one born out of convictions, and the other born out of convicts.[5] America still remains, largely, a Christian country. Australians remain, at best, a nation which believes religion is a decidedly private matter or, at worst, a nation cynical and dismissive of overt displays of faith.

If there was one word which Australians used to reflect their disdain for much of traditional religion (which really meant British Christianity), then that word was 'wowser'. This uniquely Aussie term was first coined in 1899 by a certain John Norton, who was the editor of a magazine rather inaptly called *Truth*. It was a period when a significant number of politicians were evangelical Protestants, and they were very concerned about personal morality. In that political climate some of the key legislative issues of the day concerned Sabbath observance, adultery, charity for the poor and orphans, drink and gambling, blasphemy, prostitution etc. Norton dubbed these moralizers *wowsers*, and that gave birth to a whole host of other words: 'wowserism', 'wowserites', ' wowseristic', and the verb 'to wowse'. Even Henry Lawson jumped on the bandwagon:

We must not kiss in the gardens,
We must not sing in the street,
We must not jump with a joyous shout
When a long-lost friend we meet.
We must not race by the sea-shore,
We must not sit in the sand,
We must not laugh on a New Year's Night,
For this is the Wowser's land.
(from 'The Song of the Heathen')[6]

Of course, there are sections of American culture, and their media in particular, that are scornful of conservative Christians. However, certainly in the present day, Christianity in particular has a profile and position in broader American life that could not be said of Australia. One cannot imagine an Australian Prime Minister, irrespective of his personal beliefs, announcing that he had reached decisions about public policy after prayer and consulting with his spiritual advisers. In short, one needs to be careful not to assume that trends in America are mirrored in Australia.

Nevertheless, Australia in the sixties and seventies, both deliberately and less consciously, reflected trends that were occurring on the other side of the Pacific. Indeed, the sixties witnessed the deliberate shift in Australia's allegiance from Britain to the United States. With enthusiasm Menzies followed Kennedy in committing troops to the war in Vietnam. If Australian government policy on Vietnam mirrored the policy of the US, at a street level the anti-war demonstrations "followed the American model as faithfully as the Australian government followed American policy".[7]

Similarly, the Australian 'counter-culture' movement

followed American models, as did the environmentalist movement, or the 'greenies'. Australians even attempted to model the Americans in their fascination with assassinating their political leaders, in a botched attempt to kill the Opposition leader, Arthur Calwell.

In short, while one must be cautious about assuming that American social and religious trends are repeated in the Australian context, many of the social upheavals of the sixties in America found their echoes in the urban centres of Australia.

Social analyst Hugh Mackay argues that many of the features of the epochal sixties decade, and the years that followed, emerged from a paradox in which that generation of emerging adults found itself.[8] On the one hand, they were the outcome of both a marriage boom and an economic boom. With the devastation of the war behind them, people married and had children in unprecedentedly large numbers. The 50's and 60's were also boom decades in construction, manufacturing, and mining. This was symbolized in the astonishing rise and fall of the mining company, Poseidon, whose shares rose in value from $1 to $100 between September and December 1969 (they had been worth four cents in 1966). This was a mark of the confidence in Australia's economy, particularly her mineral prospects. Unemployment was low and people were optimistic, economically, about the future.

However, the other side of the equation was that this same generation still lived under the shadow of the mushroom cloud. Prior to 1945, only God had the power to completely destroy the world; but after Hiroshima that ability fell into human hands. God's control over human events seemed diminished; man, more than ever before, was seen to control his destiny. This new generation lived with the daily reminder that Hiroshima, or something worse, could be unleashed at any moment as the two superpowers locked horns in their cold war. Dr Strangelove may have been a satire, but there was nothing humorous about the underlying political realities it was commenting upon. Mackay comments,

> The Cold War spawned an entire genre of 'despair-and-deception' ... All the rosy expectations created for the boomers were therefore tinged by a shadow: the ever-present threat of nuclear war.[9]

The sense of despair and pessimism engendered by the fear of a nuclear Armageddon was deepened by the economic downturn of the seventies. Australia's sense of economic invincibility, which pervaded the sixties, was shattered as a labour recession hit in 1974, unemployment rose, and the forecast economic nirvana did not eventuate. Most people realized that they were going to have to struggle if they were to realize the dreams of an affluent lifestyle that the consumer culture had been promising them. Prime Minister Malcolm Fraser addressed the mood of the day when he solemnly, and famously, reminded people that, "Life wasn't meant to be easy". In short, the 'selfish seventies', the 'Me' generation, continued to pursue its own self-interest, yet for many the bubble of limitless prosperity had burst, and the promises that materialism had made seemed increasingly empty and mythical.

Anti-authoritarian
While the United States and her allies, including Australia, fought a Cold War with the Soviet Bloc, there was a very real and very hot war in the villages and jungles of Southeast Asia.

The Vietnam War was widely perceived by this baby boomer generation as both a foreign war and an unjust war. Television portrayed the frighteningly graphic images of the innocent victims of this conflict. Horrific new weapons like napalm bombs were unleashed upon soldier and civilian alike. And all the while governments attempted to persuade a cynical public that this conflict was necessary to protect liberty and democracy.

While initially the Australian government had large public support for her involvement in the war, public support began to erode as the conflict escalated, and anti-war demonstrations became a regular feature of the political landscape. Indeed, the Vietnam War divided society in Australia in the same way that it split America.[10] Some presaged that it would be the most divisive issue in the country since the conscription crisis of 1916-17, except that this time the conflict wasn't along sectarian or class lines, but a conflict between generations.[11]

One of the lessons the young learnt from Vietnam was 'never trust authority'. For Americans this was underscored by the Watergate scandal. The exposure of Nixon's lies only confirmed what young Americans, in particular, had thought about those in authority. Phyllis Tickle argues that after Vietnam and Watergate,

> the individual's perception of right and wrong, do and don't do, believe and don't believe, became the litmus test for commitment and, interestingly enough, also for moral responsibility and judgement.[12]

External authorities had demonstrated their corruption and untrustworthiness. The one authority a person was left to trust was his or her own internal authority. Baby boomers were cynical and dismissive of political authority. Similarly, parental authority was challenged. In such an environment, there was little chance that religious leaders would still carry any authority. A decade later a number of high profile 'tele-evangelists' were exposed in a series of sordid sex scandals. Such humiliating revelations of hypocrisy only further reinforced the belief that religious leaders were as corrupt and self-serving as any other institutional authority.

In 1966, Beatle John Lennon famously proclaimed that the Beatles "were more popular than Jesus Christ". In context, what Lennon actually said was:

> Christianity will go. It will vanish and shrink. I needn't argue about that; I'm right and I will be proved right. We're more popular than Jesus now.[13]

The Beatles were one of the leading cultural icons of the decade, whose music and lifestyles both moulded and reflected the 60s generation.

When one places all of this in the context of a period when *Time* magazine, capturing the mood of the day, boldly announced that 'God is Dead', then we can understand why in places like Australia the proportion of adults attending church once a month or more fell from 35% to 20% during the adult lives of the boomers. Organized religion had never achieved the iron grip on the community in Australia that it had in North America, but in the sixties and seventies its moral authority declined even further, such that one commentator could proclaim "the eclipse of the church as political force within Australia".[14]

From the vantage point of the sixties itself, one may not have predicted the spiritual renaissance which was just around the corner. Mind you, the same Lennon who proudly announced the demise of Christianity was soon to be found meditating in an Ashram in India with the Maharishi Yogi. Still, it was clear that if religion were to survive, or reinvent itself, in the decades ahead, it would be a religion or spirituality that would be less ready to give its allegiance to external authorities. It would be a spirituality that looked inward for truth and guidance. It would be spirituality for whom loyalty to a given group would be less important than a commitment to follow wherever one's heart led you.

Age of freedom

In the 1960s a small group of Australians organized a 'freedom bus ride' through the Western outback of New South Wales, in order to expose people to the abuses being suffered by Aboriginal people. As with so much that young Australian people did in the sixties, this was deliberately modelled on the American experience, and the activities of civil rights workers. The sixties was the age of liberation.

Internationally, the autonomy of traditional colonial powers continued to weaken. On every front liberation movements began to emerge. In the face of the oppression of the masses in Latin America, Roman Catholic priest Gustavo Gutierrez developed a theology of liberation. Building on the writings of Simone de Beauvoir in France and Betty Friedan in America, feminist writers began to espouse women's liberation. Political liberation movements appeared throughout the world championing the causes of the downtrodden from Sri Lanka to the Basque district of Spain, and from Palestine to South America.

The development of the pill gave people, women in particular, a sexual freedom that they hadn't known before. By the end of the sixties, it was estimated that Australia had the highest per capita usage of the new contraceptive techniques.[15] People could now indulge in 'free sex' with impunity (at least until the emergence of AIDS). The era of sexual liberation was born. The only thing potentially inhibiting sexual promiscuity was the injunction of the church, an external authority. But, as we have seen, this was the age when external authorities were surrendering their hegemony over human behaviour and morals in favour of internal authorities. Besides, the clergy in Australia lacked the moral authority to stem such a tide. Debbie Boone sang an anthem for the generation when she pleaded that "it can't be wrong when it feels so right". In such a cultural climate people had freedom to experiment—with sex, with drugs, with spirituality. As Robert Wuthnow comments, "ultimately the freedom that triumphed in the 1960's was freedom to feel one's own feelings and to experience one's own sensibilities".[16]

Consumer culture

The quest for freedom on many fronts paralleled the new-found purchasing freedom that opened up to consumers during the economic boom period of the sixties. This decade saw the appearance of large supermarket chains. In 1954, a Chicago businessman, Ray Kroc, had an idea on a trip to California that would revolutionize the way people ate food, and by 1960 McDonalds restaurants were beginning to appear all across the United States. In 1968, Australia saw the first smiling, avuncular face of Colonel Sanders with his distinctive Kentucky Fried Chicken.

Wuthnow observes that Americans learnt two important lessons from these developments. Firstly, that you could shop around for some of the essential services that had always been provided at home. Secondly, that both price and convenience of access were important in choosing a product.[17] Both these factors enabled people to save two valuable commodities: money and time. The growth of consumerism, which brought with it the phenomenal range of options available to the shopper, meant that clever and effective marketing took on a new importance.

In *A Generation of Seekers*, a work which has become a standard text on the impact of the sixties on the spiritual values of Americans, Wade Clark Roof notes that, for the first time, this generation grew up with an awareness of themselves as consumers. This perception was fed by the advertisers. Advertising, Roof rightly notes, not only serves to sell products, but also promotes consumption as a way of life. From the cradle, this generation was surrounded by products created especially for them. Roof observes that new products, new toys, new commercials, and new fads were integral to the baby boom experience. People now lived under "the dictatorship of the new".[18] Further, he notes that the sixties generation's expectations of prosperity soon developed into a sense of entitlement; they had a right to interesting jobs, a large comfortable home, good times, fulfilling lives. All this led to a subtle but highly significant change in values.

Ronald Inglehart astutely argues that in times of prosperity—as opposed to economic insecurity—values tend to shift in the direction of greater concern for individual well-being, interesting experiences, quality of life, tolerance of diversity, and a greater inwardness and quest for meaning. In short, once economic survival needs are met, then higher-order needs of the self come into play to shape people's values.[19]

This can be observed on a number of fronts. Work, for example, is less and less about putting a roof over one's head and food on the table, and more about finding fulfilment and a sense of personal worth. People want to feel that somehow the work they are doing is making an impact on the world. In looking for a career, while material considerations were, and still are, important, job satisfaction was now also high on the agenda. In his 2003 Australia Day oration, playwright David Williamson noted that as human beings we want, not just to be loved, but to be respected. So, we will work longer hours and put ourselves under more stress than we can often bear in order "to purchase the symbols of success which will make one feel respected". That is why the fear surrounding loss of work is less economic, and more psychological. Unemployment or unwilling retirement or retrenchment or, that other awful word, redundancy, can be devastating to people. To have been declared redundant, expendable, no longer needed, unable to make any further worthwhile contribution, can strike at the heart of how we see ourselves. The issue is not just that we might not be able to provide for our dependants, but that we have been made to feel useless and unwanted. That is why depression, and even suicide, sometimes results from the loss of work.

Further, the age of loyalty to one company was passing. In the quest for something new, a new challenge, or a more rewarding job, people will now work for a number of firms over a period of years, or more and more will pursue self-employment. Indeed, it has been observed that having worked for one company for twenty years may even be a disadvantage when seeking new employment. What was once seen as evidence of the commendable virtues of loyalty and commitment, may in fact disguise an overly cautious personality somewhat lacking in the more desirable qualities of initiative and creativity.

It is not surprising that Christian baby boomers would have similarly loose ties to denominations or local congregations. The constant switching of allegiance from one particular Christian group to another which is more convenient or satisfying was not just a reflection of the greater mobility of society, but also another manifestation of the same quest for the new and the fulfilling that was evident in other areas of life.

In a consumer culture, where image was increasingly more important than inherent worth, it would not be long before gurus of church growth would be advising that, if a church wished to succeed in the highly competitive department store of divinity, then they should adopt the same marketing strategies that were proving so effective in the commercial world. Not surprisingly, the seeker generation spawned seeker churches, deliberately modelled, not on the synagogue, or the home, or the old-fashioned congregation, but the cinema, the shopping mall, and the drive-through, take-away, fast food outlet. In its many shapes and forms, spirituality, like hamburgers, was increasingly something one could get quickly and in a variety of places.[20]

The stressed generation

The consumer culture and its accompanying materialism offered people the instant gratification of almost all their desires. Everything was available, often 'on sale', and always 'in a store near you'. Desires soon became needs, and options soon became rights. In their quest to grasp and maintain a high standard of material comfort, boomers created the two-income family.

Further, the ethic of self-fulfilment which had usurped and conquered the old ethic of self-denial, meant that men and women wanted, and expected, more from their marriage than their parents and grandparents had. People now saw marriage as the context for meeting needs. If such needs were not met, or the relational or sexual fulfilment which people had come to demand from this partnership were not forthcoming, then to be true to oneself, divorce was seen as an unfortunate but necessary option. The changing character of the workforce, and changed perceptions about the purpose of marriage, changed the whole character of family life.

Indeed, it seemed for this generation that everything was changing. Technological progress was hard to keep up with; the new was very soon redundant. The roles of men and women were changing radically. The consumer culture promised a materialistic nirvana, but the reality was that people had to work longer hours in order to realize these dreams. Expectations for fulfilment in the workplace, the home, and in leisure activities had become, for many, unrealistic and unattainable. While more and more time-saving devices were available on the market, it just seemed that people became busier and busier. All of this, Hugh Mackay notes, created a pervasive sense of stress. This was the first generation of Australians to have identified stress as a debilitating consequence of everyday life, and to have assumed that it is a key factor, perhaps *the* key factor, in diseases and disorders ranging from heart attacks and cancer, to marriage breakdown, 'road rage' and occupational burnout.[21] It was the men of the boomers generation who succumbed to a new psychological disorder, the mid-life crisis. The question was not 'when will it strike', but 'will you be ready for it when it does?'. Such a stressed generation of people was bound to be open to solutions, no matter how bizarre, which promise, not only to relieve the stress, but to give them instantly the fulfilment and well-being that they have been taught since childhood is their innate right to enjoy.

A stressed-out generation was developing at the same time that psychologists were developing self-help therapies. Influenced by men like Carl Jung, Abraham Maslow, and Carl Rogers, practitioners emphasized that each person has the potential within himself or herself to solve their problems. Rogers, himself, taught that 'self-realization' and fulfilment could come apart from other people, traditions, or an objective God who makes moral demands.[22]

The coming of the postmodernist

A discussion of significant Western social movements in the late twentieth century would be incomplete without a brief reference to the rise of postmodernism. The new spirituality has found a fertile breeding ground in a way of thinking that dismisses objective truth in favour of a variety of truths or interpretations of the world. There are now a number of very helpful books which explain what is meant by the term 'post-modern'[23] and all we can do here is briefly and (over) simply outline its main features. We need to do this because post-modernism is the intellectual air that most of us, unwittingly, breathe and it affects how we perceive the world, and spirituality in particular.

The prefix 'post-' means 'after', and so postmodernism refers to that era after the end of the modern era. It is generally accepted that the modern era began with the Enlightenment, which itself was built on the foundations of the Renaissance. It was an era which placed man at the centre of the world. One of the great Enlightenment philosophers, Rene Descartes, began his quest for understanding with the premise that one should "doubt everything". Then, when everything is doubted, whatever is left you can be absolutely certain about. The only thing he found remaining when he had wiped the presuppositional slate clean was the certainty that he can doubt, or in the words of his famous dictum, *cogito ergo sum*—'I think, therefore I am'. As he thought about what could be known with absolute certainty, his one conclusion was that he was a thinking person. In essence, then, people are rational beings. Thus, reason became the primary avenue for understanding. No longer were things believed because of tradition, or the edicts of an authority like the church. Human reason would guide people to unravel the secrets of life and the universe, and result in certainty in one's findings.

What Descartes achieved in the philosophical world, Isaac Newton established in the scientific world. By viewing the world as a machine, whose constituent parts could be isolated and observed, one could discover both the laws that lay behind the running of this machine, and then harness this knowledge for the benefit of mankind. So began the technological revolution.

In such a rational, materialistic world, what does one do with theology? Well, the answer is that, since God is outside of the world of observable phenomena, we cannot know about him with certainty. Religion, therefore, is removed out of the world of facts, into the world of faith. Science and faith now became opposing teams, vying for the allegiance of the minds of men and women. In order to defend themselves from this rationalistic attack, religious apologists attempted to rationally defend the faith. Arguments were summoned to 'prove' the existence of God, the historicity of the resurrection, the reliability of the biblical documents. It was a case of fighting logical fire with logical fire.

That was the world of modernism. It is now maintained that this way of viewing reality is disappearing in a haze of emerging uncertainty and pluralism. Postmodernism has sprung out of a movement in literature. Traditionally, it was thought that words, either written or spoken, conveyed meaning. The words one reads in a book convey the intended meaning of the author and therefore each person who reads this book could glean the meaning, and the same right meaning from the text. In summary, we comprehend reality through the mirror of our minds, and then reflect this understanding through the mirror of language.

However, literary critics began to challenge this view, or (as the technical term is) 'deconstruct' it. Recent philosophers like Jacques Derrida argued that what we loosely describe as reality is just a way of looking at the world that has been passed on to each individual from various authority figures. Similarly, the words we use, and which we argue correspond to reality, are just socially constructed marks on a page which don't reflect some objective reality, but rather reflect the writer's own cultural context. Therefore, dictionaries are more commentaries on a culture than guides to the meanings of words. One example will illustrate the point.

In his famous *Dictionary of the English Language*, the Elizabethan Dr Samuel Johnson defined 'oats' as "a grain, which in England is generally given to horses, but in Scotland supports the people". Such a definition tells us as much about the world of Dr Johnson as it does about oats.[24] For deconstructionists, all words operate on this level. This is what is meant by words being 'social constructs'. Words tell you more about the world view of the speaker than they do the object they are purporting to correspond with.

The consequence of this way of thinking is that when reading a text, there can be no single, authoritative interpretation, simply different interpretations. It is observed that when someone writes or says something, the reality is that different people pick up different meanings from the same words. In short, meaning isn't found in the mind of the sender of a message, or in the words (or whatever codes you use to communicate your message), but in the mind of the receiver. Therefore, there are as many meanings as there are receivers. Each person will interpret reality differently. Not necessarily rightly or wrongly, just differently. For example, I might say to you, "A branch fell and hit my head". I mean by this observation, that due to the force of gravity an object fell and, unfortunately, I happened to be in its path and I must now see a medical practitioner to receive the necessary treatment to correct the damage. However, for someone else from another culture, these very same words may mean that I have offended one of the spirits, and this spirit has brought harm to me through a branch striking me, and now I must go to the local holy man to discover what sacrifice I need to offer to placate the demon I have angered. We are speaking of the same event, but with vastly different interpretations. Both these interpretations (and a potential multitude of others) point to different realities; different ways of experiencing and interpreting life. Therefore, at the heart of postmodernism is the belief that there are no absolute, universal, all-embracing truths. There is simply difference.

Consequently, pluralism is fundamental to the world of postmodernists. There are different ways of understanding, many of them no more or less valid than any others. Modernists asserted that the world is knowable; that is, that the mind can grasp the objective reality of phenomena in the world and then accurately reflect and transmit that knowledge through speech and writing. For postmodernists, a reader can no more authoritatively interpret the world, than he or she can interpret the words on a page. One reads the world through the lens of one's culture and background. What one discovers is not so much knowledge about the world, than a way of reading and interpreting what they see and experience. Further, against the claim of modernists that human reason is the path to knowledge, many today affirm that people read the world through many codes, of which reason is just one. The emotions, experience, intuition, and the spirit are all valid paths to experience and interpret reality.

Indeed, nowadays it seems that when it comes to matters of the soul, the mind and rational processes are often considered a less reliable guide to genuine spiritual encounters than experience and feelings. It appears that there is a more natural relationship between the spirit and the heart, than the spirit and the mind. The mind soon leads people into the world of propositions and creeds and dogmas, which so often strangle and smother the freedom of the spirit. On the internet one can discover a path to happiness called 'Vivation'. Vivation enables you to experience your own divine spirit, without belief systems *because your feeling awareness is more connected to your spirit than your thinking mind is.*

Given all this, postmodernists—that is, people today—talk less and less about objective truth, since what is true for one person may not be true for another. Remember, it is not interpretation, but interpretations. Postmodernists believe in a multiplicity of truths, and therefore it is better to speak of 'preference' than truth. One has preference in lifestyle, or religious belief, or sexual behaviour. Given that life is about choosing preferences, and not seeking objective truth, there is freedom to mix and match; to take the perceived best from different experiences or traditions. You can be heterosexual or homosexual, or both. Amongst Christians one often meets people who will attend an evangelical church on Sunday morning for the good teaching, and then a charismatic church in the evening for the worship, and then during the week enrol in a Cursillo retreat, for prayer, reflection, and meditation. Theologically, each of these experiences may clash, and clash quite significantly, but postmodernists are content to live with the dissonance.

Quite possibly, they have been anaesthetized to such dissonance by the nightly news bulletins on television. News shows regularly mix and match the shocking with the puerile. One moment you are watching scenes of awful human suffering as dead bodies are pulled out of a building levelled by an earthquake, and then the next item is about David Beckham's new haircut. The announcer then informs you that in the news ahead, "Twelve teenagers are killed in a terrorist bomb blast in the Middle East, and Madonna raises eyebrows with her daring new video. Stay tuned!" Most viewers are hardly conscious any more of the emotional and intellectual crunching of the gears. We are a generation comfortable with diversity.

Given the triumph of postmodernism in Western culture, it is not surprising that many of the features of the new spirituality reflect this postmodernist approach to reality.

The baby boomers, and their successors the baby busters, are today's consumers, browsing the book shops, surfing the web, looking for the right connections to wholeness and meaning. They are unlikely to surrender their autonomy to any individual or institution simply because he, she, or it might lay claim to some innate or traditional authority. They are free to choose. To experiment. To journey. They are wealthy, but their affluence has come at a price. They feel empty, disillusioned, and disconnected. It is this generation that is thirsty for spiritual water, and is prepared to taste any concoction that a vendor might offer. Given baby boomers share these common characteristics, it is not surprising that while the spiritualities for sale in the marketplace come in different shapes and sizes, many of them are plugging into the very same needs and attitudes that are features of this generation. It is to the appeal of the new spirituality that we now turn.

ENDNOTES

1   Roof, *Spiritual Marketplace*, p. 68.

2   Roof, *Spiritual Marketplace*, p. 71.

3   Os Guinness, *The Dust of Death: The Sixties Counterculture and how it Changed America Forever*, Crossway, Wheaton, 1994.

4   Donald Horne, *Time of Hope: Australia 1966-72*, Angus and Robertson, Sydney, 1979, pp. 4-7.

5   Stuart Piggin, *Evangelical Christianity in Australia: Spirit, Word and World*, Oxford University Press, Melbourne, 1996, p. 10.

6   Quoted by Piggin, *Evangelical Christianity*, pp. 51-52.

7   Geoffrey Bolton, *The Oxford History of Australia*, Vol 5, 1942-88, Oxford University Press, Melbourne, 1990, p. 170.

8   Hugh Mackay, *Generations*, Macmillan, Sydney, 1977, pp. 59-64.

9   Mackay, *Generations*, p. 61.

10 Tony Griffiths, *Contemporary Australia*, Croom Helm, London, 1977, p. 94.

11 Bolton, *The Oxford History of Australia*, p. 171.

12 Tickle, *Rediscovering the Sacred*, p. 23.

13 The Beatles, *An Anthology*, Chronicle Books, San Francisco, 2000, p. 223.

14 Maximilian Walsh, *Poor Little Rich Country: The Path to the 80's*, Penguin, Middlesex, 1979, p. 8.

15 Walsh, *Poor Little Rich Country*, p. 7.

16 Wuthnow, *After Heaven*, p. 78.

17 Wuthnow, *After Heaven*, p. 67.

18 Wade Clark Roof, *A Generation of Seekers: The Spiritual Journeys of the Baby Boomer Generation*, Harper, San Francisco, 1993, p. 43.

19 Quoted by Roof, *A Generation of Seekers*, p. 43.

20 Wuthnow, *After Heaven*, p. 67.

21 Mackay, *Generations*, p. 65.

22 See Collins, *The Soul Search*, p. 51.

23 For example, David Dockery (ed.), *The Challenge of Postmodernism*, Bridgepoint Books, Wheaton, 1995; Stanley J Grenz, *A Primer on Postmodernism*, Eerdmans, Grand Rapids, 1996.

24 See the helpful discussion in Kevin J. Vanhoozer, *Is There a Meaning in This Text?* Zondervan, Grand Rapids, 1998, chapter 2.

Chapter 4

The Appeal of Spirituality

Running on empty

The cover story of the Sydney *Sunday Telegraph's* 'Sunday Magazine' featured a story on "The life, lurves (sic), and spirituality" of model, actress and, most famously of all, ex-Mrs Mick Jagger, Jerry Hall.[1] In discussing how she sees her life now, the article reports that Hall uses the word 'spiritual' a lot. Having a baby by natural childbirth was "very spiritual", as was the experience of watching her god-daughter being born. She calls her love of poetry spiritual. She even describes her ability to forgive the press for the dreadful things they have said about her and Jagger as a spiritual thing. It would be very hard to define what Hall means by spiritual, but whatever it is, it is important to her.

Spirituality is important to more and more people nowadays. Is this just a contemporary fad? Is this just another example of the human being's propensity to conform to the behaviour of the crowd? Once prominent and respected people begin to speak openly about their spirituality, then is it just a matter of the rest of us joining the chorus, obediently singing the same sacred tune?

There may be an element of this in the new phenomenon. However, others suggest that the contemporary quest for the sacred is really an overdue, and thoroughly expected, response of people who are innately spiritual beings to the suppression of their natural spiritual desires and yearnings by a philosophically and economically materialistic culture. For decades marketers have sought to persuade people that 'Coke Adds Life', and that financial independence and security is the path to peace and happiness. We have already noted that while it was the 1960's which saw the development of the consumer culture, this very expansion served, ultimately, to show people that they had been sold a lie. On a hot day, carbonated soft drinks look and taste cold and refreshing. Yet, within minutes, the thirst returns and the parched throat cries out for something real and satisfying, not synthetic and phoney.

For many observers on the rise of spirituality the spirituality phenomenon is best explained as being a welcome and understandable response to the increasing secularization of Western society. In the midst of an increasingly materialistic society we should not be surprised that many people have a growing sense that the consumer culture which promised so much, has woefully failed to satisfy people's deepest needs. David Tacey, comments,

> I think many people feel that we are running on empty, our spiritual fuel gauge having registered 'low' for some time. Warning signals are evident in all walks of life: depression is now so prevalent that some one in five Australians suffers from acute or chronic, often undiagnosed depression.[2]

Along with depression, Tacey cites the incidence in our society of chronic fatigue and burnout, the breakdown of family structures, instability in the work place, the widespread abuse of drugs and alcohol, and the increase in suicide. He sees these social problems as manifestations of a spiritual illness in the wider community. He argues that increasing numbers of young people are turning to spirituality as a desperate attempt to stem the encroaching tide of destructive materialism.

However, as we have seen, the new spirituality is not just a reaction to the consumer culture, it is also a *product* of a commodity culture. The seismic sixties both created the hunger for the spiritual that would eventually manifest itself in the new spirituality, but also set the contours for what this new spirituality would look like. It would be a spirituality that would appeal to the people of that generation.

As commentators like Roof, Wuthnow, and Tacey point out, this new spirituality is wide and diverse. Some of it eschews any connection with what is traditionally referred to as 'religion'. Much of it is 'pseudo-religious', being a syncretistic meshing of some of the more appealing elements from various traditional faiths, spiced up with ingredients drawn from modern self-help therapies. Others who have been awakened to spiritual experiences have done so within the context of orthodox Christian belief. These various spiritual groups differ widely, both in what they believe, and in how they express their faith. Nevertheless, when one surveys the broad expanse of contemporary spiritualities, it is striking how much they share. Again and again one finds, in particular, the same needs mentioned that spirituality is required to meet.

We have seen that devotees of the new spirituality are largely baby boomers, and their offspring the Baby Busters, and the social changes they have lived through have profoundly influenced their world view. They look at life, social relationships, values and behaviours, and themselves differently from the generations before them. While each of these people are individuals, with their own unique life story, they have all been subject to the same events that have moulded their life and times, and therefore they have much in common.

To this generation of spiritual seekers, what is the appeal of the new spirituality? Which aspects of it hit a familiar and friendly chord with many of them? We will now turn to examine the themes that reappear in many of the writings on spirituality, keeping in mind that these are not qualities of each and every kind of spirituality. All spiritualities will contain some, indeed most, of these features. Some will contain all of them. Put together they present a mosaic of the character of the spirituality of our day. These are the key features of those spiritualities that seek to connect to today's spiritual seeker. These are the things that people are looking for as they search for connection and wellbeing.

1. Hunger for relationship

Each Friday my son brings home the weekly 'Head Master's Bulletin', from the nearby Anglican school which he attends. In one issue, there was a brief extract from a consultant's report on the role that Chapel plays in the pastoral care of the students. The report notes that, "The boys understand that Chapel offered them an opportunity to explore the link between *their spirituality and daily life,* providing them with a sense of *spiritual connectedness*" (italics mine).

The school is avowedly religious, and Christian principles undergird its policies. It is interesting, therefore, that neither of these words, 'religion' or 'Christianity', are used by the consultants (who were, it must be said, outsiders invited to analyse the school) to describe this dimension of the school's ministry. It may well be that 'spirituality' is preferred because this is the more inclusive term. While some of the boys may not claim allegiance to any particular religion, nor would they say that the Christian faith is their faith, presumably very few would take exception to a statement that implied that the school was assisting them in a growing awareness of their spirituality. More particularly, this spirituality, whatever it is, is tied up with a sense of 'connect-edness' to what is around them. If there is one word, more than any other, which has become the identifying mark of the new spirituality it is the term **connectedness**. What is meant by this term, and what lies behind it?

The influential Anglican theologian D. B. Knox outlined what was one of the cardinal tenets of his doctrine of God. He wrote,

> The doctrine of the Trinity is the glory of the Christian religion. It tells us that ultimate reality is personal rela-tionship. God is ultimate reality, and is the ground of all other reality, and yet God is not a single monad or an impersonal absolute, but God is a relationship.[3]

God, in essence, is Father, Son, and Spirit, each in eternal rela-tionship with the other, without ever compromising the essen-tial oneness of the divine being. Since God in his essence is relationship, it follows that love is also fundamental and inte-gral to his being. As John writes, "anyone who does not love does not know God, for God is love" (1 John 4:8). Given that we are made in the image of God, it follows then that for us, also, what is ultimate in life is personal relationships. Knox rightly argues that relationships are the most real things there are.

One is not surprised, then, to find at the very heart of the new spirituality a hunger for relationship, both with God and with other people. This quest for relationship is often not expressed in precisely this way. As we have seen, most writers on spirituality prefer the term 'connectedness'. David Tacey argues that, today, spirituality is primarily about connected-ness with nature and the cosmos; it "often expresses itself as an emotional relationship with an invisible sacred presence".[4]

For example, Jeffrey Sobosan in his book on the spirituality of animal care relates the story of an old priest who had a canary as a companion for eleven years. He always left the canary's cage door open so that it had free access to the rooms of the apartment. One day while the priest was reading in his rocking chair he tilted back and crushed the canary. Two days later Sobosan recalls talking to this priest, who shared what *his brother* had meant to him. The use of the term 'brother' for the canary spoke powerfully to Sobosan who, in his book, makes a plea for humans to recognize their kinship with the animal world. For him, the whole earth is composed of kindred beings; it is a holy family.[5]

We have already mentioned Shannon Jung's experience of relatedness to the sheep she observed on the Colorado Mountains. This experience of relationship is not confined to animate objects. Jung cites the testimony of a rock climber whose senses were filled with the aliveness of the environment. The touch of the rock face, the sounds of the birds and the cascading water evoked in him a spiritual serenity. He commented, "I began to talk to the rock in an almost audible, childlike way, as if the rock were my friend".[6] Similarly, David Tacey cites one of his students who recalled,

> once, in the outback with a group of friends, I had a powerful sensation of the earth as a living, breathing being, with myself connected to it as a smaller being. This feeling of aliveness extended to the galaxies above, and to the night sky teeming with points of starry light. This changed my perspective on everything.[7]

While traditional Christian theology has recognized that we have a relationship with the created order, and one which ought to be a caring and benevolent custodianship, nevertheless this relationship is not personal. Only with other human beings and, ultimately, with God himself is our hunger for relationship satisfied. However when environmental spiritualists like Jung speak of their 'friendship with' the universe this is much more than metaphor. For them, the universe is 'human-friendly', and an organism with which we can be in spiritual communion, if only we will open ourselves up to the possibility.

This relatedness to the world may then lead to relationships with other parts of the creation, in particular other human beings. For example, the common discovery of a communion with nature can lead to the establishment of faith communities; one now finds oneself in relationship with others who have shared the same spiritual experience. Indeed, one of the appeals of the new spirituality is that, however your personal experience of the spirit might manifest itself, you are almost inevitably joined into a community of like-minded people. Feminist spirituality produces a sisterhood bound together by their common experience of the woman spirit. Exploring aboriginal spirituality doesn't just give you a sense of kinship with the sacred land, but with others who are moved and energized by this same encounter.

This hunger for relationship is common to virtually all people. It is poignantly portrayed in the Tom Hanks film, *Cast Away*, which tells the story of a man marooned on a tiny Pacific Island for over four years, with no human company. He paints a face on a volleyball which he names Wilson, and then seeks to relate to it. Intellectually he is aware of the absurdity of talking to a ball, but so deep is his hunger for relationship that he submerges this knowledge and creates a sense of companionship with this make-believe friend.

When Wilson is set adrift at sea during a storm, the castaway is heartbroken and desolate. While this film is not a parable of the human condition, there is a sense in which many people today feel like castaways, disconnected, and cut off from meaningful and satisfying relationships. The amazing growth of supportive small groups testifies to the need that people feel for supportive, sustaining relationships. On the reason for this quest for community, Wade Clark Roof perceptively writes:

> [T]he small-group movement of recent years emerged out of the breakdown of traditional support structures. A weakening of families, of ethnic and religious ties, of community and other dislocations of a highly mobile society are all factors. Networks now replace neighbourhoods as a primary sphere of social interaction. Electronic communication is a medium through which a growing amount of human exchange occurs. Consequently, people find that many of their emotional and support needs go increasingly unmet; or in order to meet them, they must turn to new types of bondings and communities focused around, most notably, self-expression and nurturance, group sharing, and helping others. It may even be that the very notion of community itself is undergoing a fundamental change. For whatever reason, people seem to be more intentional and deliberate about the communities they create—they choose to 'make' community, so to speak. They do so when they consciously select a congregation to join, commit themselves to spend a week with Habitat for Humanity, go on-line to share evangelical

faith with others a continent away, or participate in a goddess spirituality workshop.[8]

One of the most obvious marks of all contemporary spiritualities is an avowed longing for connection.

2. Thirst for experience

Inextricably tied to the hunger for relationship is the universal desire for spiritual experience. Whatever shape a person's spirituality takes today, it is almost always both a reaction to, or rejection of, that way of living and responding to God which is formal, institutional and cerebral. Instead, people are looking for a relationship with God (or the cosmos, or whatever) which is real, spontaneous, and profoundly experiential.

We have already seen that Stephanie Dowrick describes the spirituality of today as "freelance spirituality". Writing in the 'Good Weekend' of *The Sydney Morning Herald*, she maintains that this kind of spirituality has understandably developed at the same time that social changes have led to a new valuing of individual experience. For Stephanie Dowrick, "spirituality is, above everything else, a personal experience that cannot be imposed. It arises out of and reflects a *lived* sense that there is dimension to human existence that goes beyond the explicable and mundane".[9] This dimension can be known and experienced. Indeed, this knowledge may, itself, be fundamentally experiential, and not one which can be easily articulated or put into words.

Even when the object of one's search is not a personal being like the God and Father of Jesus Christ, ultimately people are still looking for an encounter that will deeply touch their soul. According to Blanca Greenberg the journey to spiritual self-discovery often begins with subtle spiritual experiences like the "quiet whispers of the trees and the serenity that you *feel* as you walk through a forest, the *warm feeling* of joy and promise that you *experience* as you watch the sunset, or the *overwhelming feeling* of discovery and *ecstasy* that you encounter as you watch a rainbow develop in the midst of stormy weather".[10] The resonance one feels with the cosmos in one's soul at such times is the key to spiritual understanding. All these encounters with the world touch one's soul and are seen, therefore, as spiritual.

Even for those who have not rejected organized religion, there is a perception that much of religion today, including evangelical religion, is seriously defective. Something basic and essential is missing. For example, the introduction to Bruce Demarest's celebrated book, *Satisfy Your Soul: Restoring the Heart of Christian Spirituality*, begins by posing these questions:

When was the last time you knew you were in the presence of the Lord? When did you last sense His strong hand directing you? Hear the voice of the Spirit that speaks, in the words of the psalmist, as deep calling to deep?

As Christians we are promised the indwelling presence of God, by the Spirit. What we hunger for is an encounter, strong and genuine, with God—and more than that, a way to be filled from within every day, a way to know we are accompanied by Him and not left on our own.

But is that our experience? For many—possibly for you—it is not.[11]

Much of the appeal of the medieval mystics to Christians today is that here were men and women who clearly had this 'something' that today many testify is missing from their spiritual lives. The likes of Patrick of Ireland, Francis of Assisi, or St Benedict, all spoke and taught of practising the presence of God. It is thought that while their theology may have lacked the finely-tuned precision of a Luther or a Calvin, they evidenced a dynamic reality in their relationship with God that the Reformers missed. Indeed, some would argue that it was this very concern for theological exactness that eventually took the heart out of Christian faith and piety. At one time, the spiritual was the realm of the daily experience of the presence of God; then it became the domain of verbal creedal confessions. Today, more and more evangelicals are asserting that we need to rediscover that which has been lost, and perhaps the mystics are the ones to guide us in this search. But more of this in a later chapter.

The phenomenal worldwide growth of the pentecostal/ charismatic movement, and the significant inroads it has made into traditional Protestant and Catholic churches, is due more to its emphasis on experience than any other factor. Fuller Seminary New Testament professor, Russell Spittler, in his analysis of the core values of pentecostalism asserts that, "Nothing matters more to pentecostals than their own personal experience with God. The measure of the genuineness of an encounter with God is the tangible, conspicuous presence of deep feeling".[12]

At the heart of charismatic spirituality is worship. This is why charismatics go to church, and worship is the central event of the gathering. It is in the act of worship that charismatics encounter and experience the divine. As Daniel

Albrecht points out, for them worship is a code word for the 'presence of God'. He maintains that worship involves a deep communion between divinity and humanity, an encountering, a mutual experiencing.[13]

Increasingly, Christians are asserting that the faith which has been bequeathed to them is barren and unsatisfying, and unless we recapture the experiential dimension of our faith, then the bogus spiritualities of the world will attract and woo our membership. David Tacey counsels the church that its survival and future lies with a return to the mystical and experiential. He cites a conversation between a follower of the New Age and a Catholic. The latter explained how his church was attempting to modernize by placing greater emphasis on the rational and moral basis of the faith, and less on its rites and mysteries. The New Ager commented that he found this odd, because these were the very elements that made New Age spirituality so appealing to him and others.[14]

In short, whether one's spirituality is of the New Age variety, or is feminist, or environmental, Catholic, charismatic, or evangelical, the search is on for an encounter which reaches beyond the mind, and touches the heart, the emotions, and the deep recesses of the human soul. This is the spirituality which today's seekers are looking for, and those who offer such an experience receive a sympathetic hearing. For many people, spirituality is not about what you believe, but what you feel. It is born and is nurtured viscerally, not intellectually. If people feel empty in today's materialistic world, then the remedy is a feeling of peace, satisfaction and connectedness. As Shannon Jung, in bold type, proclaims, **To be authentic, the spirituality we seek must be one that we feel in our bones.**

3. Non-rational

Most people today no longer accept that reason is the only sustainable path to truth. Indeed, modern Western history has demonstrated again and again that reason and technology have brought the world to the brink of a man-made Armageddon. Any good that the Age of Reason has done for the world, is well and truly matched by the evil it has unleashed.

Given the centrality of experience in contemporary spirituality, it is not surprising that genuine spiritual events or encounters are said to often occur outside the realm of the intellectual or the verbal. The website, 'joy2meu', maintains that truth is not an intellectual concept. Rather,

> truth is an emotion, something that I feel within ... It is that 'AHA' feeling. The feeling of a light bulb going on in my head. That 'Oh, I get it' feeling. The intuitive feeling when something just feels right ... or wrong. It's that gut feeling, the feeling in my heart.

Health Care specialist John Shea, in the context of arguing for spirituality to be seen as an integral component of health care, writes that spirituality is "a subtle something", whose "primary languages are imaginative and evocative, seeking to help people recognize the spiritual in their midst".[15]

One may not be able to understand or explain a spiritual encounter, but that in no way invalidates it. The historical monotheistic faiths, in particular, are criticized for their over-emphasis on the rational and propositional character of their spirituality. For faiths like Christianity, the spiritual is the realm of creeds, confessions, sermons, catechisms and theologies. In Islam, the first sound a child is to hear, and the last words uttered to a dying person are the words of the

Shahadah ("there is no God but God and Muhammad is his prophet"). A creed. It is argued that such things are not illegitimate, simply inadequate if they are seen to be the essence of what a spiritual encounter might be. The stirrings and connectings of the human spirit cannot be so circumscribed. Spiritual experiences often transcend the rational. This does not mean they must be *ir*rational, but that they are not validated or invalidated by prior theological commitments. In fact, it is argued that one of the attractions of the new spirituality is that it does not ask for proofs; "the proof is in the experience itself".[16]

We have already made mention of the resurgence of interest in mysticism within the Christian tradition. Part of the appeal of the mystics lies in the fact that they offer an encounter with the divine which goes beyond the rational and opens up other dimensions of the human personality as avenues for divine experience. For example, in her bestseller, *The Cloister Walk*, Kathleen Norris describes her introduction to the discipline of 'spiritual reading'. In her own words this approach is "an attempt to read more with the heart than with the head. One does not try to 'cover' a certain amount of material so much as to surrender to whatever word or phrase catches the attention".[17]

4. Non-judgemental

In his book *The Dance of Wounded Souls*, Robert Burney recounts that when he first came to the self-help programme entitled 'Joy2meu', he would not even use the word 'God' because he had been spiritually, emotionally, and mentally abused in childhood with a concept of God that was vengeful and punishing. I had my sexuality abused by a shame-based religion that taught me that God would send me to burn in hell forever for even thinking about sex.

For a man keenly aware that he was a spiritual being, and yet carrying with him this baggage of guilt and fear, what kind of spirituality could he connect with? His answer was that, "I started to try to find a concept of a Higher Power that could possibly love me and be on my side". The theological conclusions he has drawn, and which he now offers spiritual seekers, are that "Humans are not bad or shameful. There was no original sin. The human condition and the evolution of human nature have been dictated by planetary conditions and are a perfect part of the Divine Plan".[18]

This is a recurrent theme in much contemporary spirituality, especially of the New Age variety. God does not judge us. An encounter with the Other who is kind and loving, never produces fear. Spiritual experiences ought not to produce a sense of guilt, but a sense of worth and of being unconditionally loved. It is often maintained that religions, and especially Christianity, have sought to maintain adherence and promote conformity by requiring credal orthodoxy, and by threatening members with dire warnings of eternal punishment for anyone who strays from the party line and follows the free and independent flow of their spirit. People today do not like restrictions placed upon them. They hate being told what to do. They want to be helped and affirmed, not criticized and judged. Self-help teacher, Louise Hay, sings a song that would soothe the soul of any troubled seeker when she writes,

Remember, though, that life never, ever, ever judges. It's almost like life, God, the universe always says "yes" to whatever we choose to believe.[19]

In 1992, Jean Eadie published her reminiscences of 'dying' some twenty years before when, for five hours, after haemorrhaging during a hysterectomy, she went to the world beyond. Now that she has been there and come back she can report that there is no future judgement, and hell is nothing more than the momentary suffering we feel when we realize, during our life review, that we have caused grief to others. Further, sin is not something bad, but an opportunity to learn. About Jesus, she writes that, "he was aware of all my sins and faults but all that didn't matter right now. He just wanted to hold me and share his love with me".[20]

One of the more interesting features of the modern spirituality phenomenon is the renewed interest in angels. Both New Age gurus and evangelical preachers have rediscovered the importance of the ministry of angels. In America more people claim to believe in angels today than a decade ago, with national studies suggesting that about one-third of all Americans claim to have had a personal encounter with an angel.[21] Angels appear to mortals from time to time in the Bible and almost invariably it is a terrifying encounter. When Zechariah is confronted by an angel while burning incense in the temple, Luke records that, "he was troubled when he saw him, and fear fell upon him" (Luke 1:12). It seems, though, that over the past two thousand years angels have undergone a dramatic image overhaul, and for today's baby boomer generation the Lord God only sends user-friendly angels. Robert Wuthnow observes that, as depicted in popular books and in our interviews, angels never scold. They give unconditional love. They have a good sense of humour ... (and) make no demands and require no continuing relationship. Moreover, they are uninterested in theological arguments, preferring just to perform random acts of kindness.[22]

Given the unease many people feel with a spirituality that is judgemental, it is not surprising that the contemporary church has softened its earlier 'hardline' approach. According to researcher George Barna, as many as one-fifth of all American churches have adopted some version of the 'seeker service' in order to attract outsiders to church. This model of church growth has been exported to other countries, and many pastors in Australia, if they haven't embraced it in totality, nevertheless have sought to adapt it to their own context. It operates out of a missionary paradigm, attempting to bridge the gulf between the secular materialistic society in which it finds itself, and a church that is widely perceived as being boring, irrelevant and judgemental. While seeker churches form part of the evangelical Christian constituency, and most seeker pastors affirm orthodox Christian truths, these churches tend to proclaim a message that is 'soft' and non-judgemental. While the holiness and purity and sovereignty of God is not denied, and even affirmed, it is the love, mercy, and faithfulness of God which is emphasized. From his observation of many seeker churches, Kimon Sargeant concludes that the God they proclaim is "not an angry father, eager to judge and condemn. Instead, God is an understanding compassionate father."[23]

Sargeant argues that seeker churches are successful

because they do not condemn the world of modern culture. He quotes a sermon on divorce by Willow Creek's senior pastor, Bill Hybels, in which he says that, "there is not an ounce of judgement in my spirit for those of you who are going through or who are recovering from divorce in your family ... You matter to God more than you realize you do".[24] Tellingly, a George Barna survey of weekend participants at Willow Creek found that while 91% stated that their highest value in life was having a deep personal relationship to God, of this same group 25% of singles, 38% of single parents, and 41% of divorced individuals "admitted having illicit sexual relationships in the last six months".[25]

5. Inclusive

In offering a spirituality for agnostics and atheists, Robert Burney maintains that any person has an absolute right to believe whatever he or she chooses to believe. He goes on to say, "If you choose to believe in a punishing, judgemental, male god, that is your total right and privilege. If that works for you great. It does not work for me".[26] It would be hard to find a statement that better typifies the inclusive spirit of today. Once truth is dispensed with, then what remains is preference. Once God is no longer at the centre, then the human being and his or her rights and desires become sovereign. Once spirituality is cut loose from any confessional basis then the truth of an experience becomes self-validating. One can discover one's own private and personal spirituality. The issue is not so much one of truth or virtue, but it is simply utilitarian; it works for you. I have no right to judge what works for you. My only obligation is to respect the diversity of beliefs and experiences and to affirm you in what gets you through the night.

Pluralism has won the day in the Western world. The reality of cultural pluralism, that is, the obvious fact that people of different backgrounds think, believe and behave differently, has given birth to philosophical pluralism. It is accepted that these differences are simply culturally determined ways of responding to reality, which have gradually developed over centuries. One has no right to pronounce judgement on another's view of reality unless, of course, that view of reality hurts or impedes your own freedom of expression. Instead, one ought to affirm the rightness of a particular belief or experience for that individual who benefits from it. Indeed, if one approaches this diversity with the appropriate open mind, then one might find one's own world view, or spirituality, enriched through exposure to, and contact with, the experiences of others.

So, today, it is thought that one can grow spiritually by tapping into the spiritual traditions and experiences of others. Some time ago I met a young Anglican clergyman. Each weekday morning he attends the daily eucharist at the church in which he ministers and he finds the event deeply satisfying. Often on Saturdays he will visit a Buddhist monastery in the hills behind the city where he lives, and join the monks there in quiet contemplation. He is spiritually enriched through these diverse encounters of the one Real or Divine or Other which energizes them all. For him, ministry is not dogmatically asserting that the path on which he walks is one that each person must walk or face some kind of eternal censure. He is on a journey of spiritual self-discovery and growing self-awareness. Your journey may be along a different path and, indeed, may have a different destination. But if you wish to walk with him on his journey, or if the paths you both walk along should intersect, then you can walk and grow together.

It would be surprising if the spirit of inclusivism, which is now so pervasive in Western society, did not affect the spirituality of evangelical Christians. Less and less are evangelicals comfortable with exclusive claims to salvation. Both at the popular level, and the scholarly level, conservative Christians increasingly are persuaded that the devout believer of any religion will be saved on the last day, albeit through the atoning blood of Christ. Kimon Sargeant argues that it is in response to pluralism that most seeker churches play down God's judgement in their sermons, focusing instead on God's paternal love. Their messages, he observes, demonstrate an ethic of civility and tolerance. He goes on to note,

> In sum, seeker churches introduce seekers to the Christian message by presenting the exclusivist theology of evangelicalism in the friendly guise of an egalitarian, fulfilment-enhancing, fun religious encounter with God. As a result, seeker church pastors make orthodox theology less offensive and more civil for a pluralistic society.[27]

Similarly, hell is not denied, just rarely mentioned. Very few evangelical churches nowadays present hell as the abode of the unrighteous and a place of conscious, eternal torment (even less so, given the growing acceptance of annihilation as a more appropriate, and certainly more culturally acceptable, description of the fate of the wicked). Hell is more often described in terms of being "a Christless eternity". Certainly, for those who know Christ, the prospect of eternity without him would be a terrible loss, but for those who have lived a

Christless temporality with no apparent concern, it is a rather benign way to describe eternal condemnation.

6. Everyday spirituality

Utilizing the jargon that is so common today, John Shea, in a discussion of the character of the soul, writes:

> On the one hand, the soul is the primordial connectedness of the human person with the Sacred, or Spirit, or God (or with whatever other words denote Ultimate Reality). On the other hand, soul points to the connection of the human person with the mind-body organism and through the organism with the entire world.[28]

Traditionally, many people have thought of spirituality as a deeply personal thing; an individual's private search for meaning and fulfilment. While, indeed, it appears that some of the spiritualities 'for sale' in the supermarket of the sacred are of the fast food type, requiring little commitment of time or self, this would not be a true characterization of all contemporary spirituality. Authentic spirituality, it is said, may be one that comes to birth deep within the individual, but it cannot remain simply an inner experience. David Tacey notes,

> Although we might initially discover the spirit within ourselves, in quiet introspection, retreat, seclusion or introversion, once spirit is contacted it brings with it an imperative to go outside ourselves and serve others and the world. If we confine the spirit within our own subjectivity, we are liable to explode from the build-up of impossible energy that cannot find fulfilment.[29]

It is recognized that the connections one's spirit makes with other kindred spirits is seen to have ethical ramifications. For example, an encounter with the spirit of the cosmos, which infuses every thing, animate and inanimate, must result in a sense of responsibility to protect and care for the environment. A discovery of the richness of aboriginal spirituality should produce an active concern for the injustices faced by indigenous peoples in our community. A woman's recognition of her relationship to the Earth goddess will result in a commitment to further liberate other women from the shackles of patriarchal oppression.

Further, it is recognized that the spiritual is not only an essential part of our humanity, but that it is indissolubly connected with the rest of life. Interest in the spiritual is emerging in the corporate world, the world of athletics, and in social justice. For example, businesses are now recognizing that it is in their best interest to have a concern, not just for the physical, mental, and social wellbeing of their employees, but also their spiritual wellbeing. Indeed, those employees who are holistically healthy tend to be more productive. John Shea quotes the findings of one quantitative and qualitative study of business executives, which discovered that spirituality was one of the most important determinants of these executives' organizational performance, and that those who were more highly developed spiritually achieved better results.[30] Similarly, those involved in health care recognize that the kind of healing that is simply focused on the health of the body is too narrow. Physical ill health affects also the mind, and has social ramifications as well. More than that, ill health also impacts a person's spiritual wellbeing. Consequently, there is a greater emphasis on holistic therapies, and experts in spirituality are increasingly seen as having a vital role to play in the healing process.

All of this, in turn, leads to a belief that authentic spirituality is one that pervades every area of life, seven days a week. One increasingly finds amongst evangelical writers a concern that, for too long, the piety of evangelical Christianity has been too removed from everyday life. Sermons are perceived to be fine, exegetical analyses of the meaning of the ancient scriptures, yet often with little attention given to how these scriptures equip people to live Monday to Friday. It is maintained that the churches which are growing today are those that have made relevance the first principle in the preaching and teaching programme of the church. It is recognized that there are six other days in the Christian's week, and that unless a church can instruct and support people who face the demands of everyday life, then this generation of spiritual shoppers will take themselves to those churches which can do that.

7. Marketplace spirituality

'Shop the web for spirituality' advertises the internet. It really is an astonishing concept that an encounter with the divine is now for sale, conveniently located, and available at the swipe of a MasterCard. We have seen that the economic boom of the sixties saw the explosion of the consumer culture, which in turn created a consumer mentality. Advertising is now pandemic. From the backside of shopping dockets to the jerseys of football teams, from writing in the sky to the daily junk mail in the letter box, people are constantly confronted by the lure of the marketplace. Everything is available, just a credit card's transaction away. We have gradually been convinced that this marketplace exists for the satisfaction of our needs and desires. Such a culture has produced a generation which now sees self-fulfilment as one of its inalienable rights.

Theologian David Wells has argued that the dominance of the marketplace has meant that there are now two ideas at the centre of capitalistic society. Firstly, the audience is sovereign. Secondly, that ideas find legitimacy and value only within the marketplace.[31] In other words, an idea or belief no longer has any intrinsic value; rather it is given value by the consumer, and usually on the basis of its perceived usefulness for living.

Inevitably, this mindset has deeply affected spirituality. Approvingly, John Shea reflects this understanding when he argues that people's spiritual interests arise out of their spiritual needs. Today's spiritual seeker knows what she wants and what she does not want. This spiritual hunger "is looking for a specific menu. Spiritual interest decides which spiritualities or parts of spiritualities will be adopted and which will not be pursued".[32]

Given that each spiritual shopper is looking for a specific menu, increasingly spiritualities are tailored today to meet the needs and desires of the customer. We have seen that the various religious and pseudo-religious organizations that comprise the so-called 'New Age' offer a variety of courses and therapies ultimately aimed at improving the individual's well-being. The needs of the self are supreme, and these needs can be met through tapping into the divine, connecting with the energy in the cosmos, or learning from the secrets of the ages.

In a society where the consumer is sovereign, it is not surprising that theologically conservative churches have also looked to the marketplace for their models for church growth. One of the most successful exponents of this is North America's Willow Creek Community Church, which Fortune magazine praised in 1989 as "the paradigm of customer orientation".[33] Willow Creek, which has influenced thousands of churches in America and around the world, has consciously tailored its services to meet the felt needs of the baby boom generation. It is a marketing masterpiece.

To a stressed-out generation, facing emotional burnout, and which has been weaned and fed on consumerism, a spirituality that is needs-focussed will find a ready audience. Today, when a Christian is asked why he or she attends a particular church, frequently the answer is a variation on the theme that, "this church meets my spiritual needs". Once, a church could have relied on the loyalty of its members. Now, in a highly competitive environment, it is believed that, like any other seller, a church needs to market its religious product both to attract new members, but also to keep the old ones who may be tempted to move to another church with a more attractive programme.

Rick Warren is pastor of one of America's largest churches, Saddleback Community Church. Having found that traditional methods of church growth had failed, Warren revamped his approach. His highly influential book *The Purpose Driven Church* explains his strategy for church growth. Fundamental to his new approach was targeting people's needs. For Warren, ministry is all about meeting needs in Jesus' name. Seeking to justify his emphasis biblically he looks to Jesus as the model of a human needs-based preacher. Indeed, Christ's preaching showed a "total emphasis on felt needs and hurts".[34] In his initial promotional brochure, Warren advertised "a new church designed to meet your needs", and concluded with the slogan, "Discover the Difference!" It is a church where a person can "Meet new friends", "Enjoy upbeat music", and

"Hear positive, practical messages which encourage you each week". The absence of the word 'God' from the brochure is as striking as is the absence of sin (or any of its parallelisms) from the opening of the vision statement. Warren acknowledges that he has made some "small concessions" to American culture in matters of taste and style. He knows his culture and knows it is consumer-driven, and to such a culture he has designed a religious product that is attractive and saleable. Indeed, taking on board the supreme optimism of capitalistic American culture, Warren confidently affirms that anybody can be won to Christ if you discover the key to his or her heart. In other words, with the right product and the right packaging, you can entice any purchaser.

Further, the marketplace has not just determined much of the style and focus of contemporary spirituality, it has also set the terms in which the success of any spirituality is measured. In short, it is quantitative. The guru of church growth marketing strategy, George Barna, argues that for the local church to be a successful business it must impact a growing share of its market area.[35] In other words, the goal of marketing Christianity is spoken of less in terms of that which promotes the glory of God, but in terms of numerical growth, quantified in graphs, tables, and statistics.

8. Therapeutic

Closely linked with a consumer-oriented spirituality, tailor-made for the marketplace, is a spirituality designed to heal an individual's brokenness, be it physical, emotional, psychological, or social. The website 'Vivation' opens its web page with the promise that the spirituality it offers "permanently resolves pain, stress, and negative emotions". Theologian David Wells has observed that in every part of society, including the church, we are witnessing the triumph of the therapeutic over the moral.[36]

The emphasis today, in all kinds of spirituality, is on feeling good about yourself. Listen to the following:

> It's time to relax and become comfortable around your money. You need to stretch yourself and position yourself right out of your comfort zone. For example, it may involve a little exercise like putting on your best clothes and ordering coffee in a fancy restaurant or hotel lobby. Even though you could make the coffee for half the price at home, the total experience may enlarge your thinking. You may even feel better about yourself and your life.

This sounds like a quote from a popular infotainment television programme, or some advice from one of the many 'get-rich-quick' paperbacks that you can pick up at your local bookseller and newsagent. Instead, it's 'biblical wisdom' from Brian Houston, the pastor of one of Australia's largest and best known churches, Hillsong.[37] It is not hard to see the appeal of such advice to a self-centred baby boomer generation.

Houston maintains that part and parcel of becoming a 'money magnet', and obtaining the financial prosperity that God has planned for each of his children, is having a healthy self-image. He argues that, "If you say, 'I'll never live in a beautiful house like that', then you probably never will. It has a lot to do with the way you see yourself and the way you think God sees you".[38] In words drawn right out of the world of self-help therapy, Houston encourages his readers to: Lift your self-worth, Increase your skills, Build your credibility, and asks, Do you know your limitations?

9. An immanental, inner-directed spirituality

It is not surprising that much of the new spirituality, whether it draws its inspiration from Eastern religions or occult traditions, or from orthodox Christian beliefs, tends to emphasize the immanence of God over against his transcendence. The Bible presents God as being essentially transcendent, that is, his being transcends this world. He is known because he has chosen to reveal himself, but as creator and sustainer of his world he is separate from it. What is more, the rebellion of men and women has further served to distance man and God. Where once they walked together in the garden in the cool of the day, now he is hidden behind his impenetrable holiness.

Jesus said, "No one has ever seen God; the only God, who is at the Father's side, he has made him known" (John 1:18). If this verse speaks of God's otherness and transcendence, it also tells of his immanence. The distant, hidden God has come amongst us and has done so in his Son. He is Immanuel, God with us. Further, this transcendent God remains with us, just as he promised (Matt 28:20), and does so by his Spirit. Those who believe in this God through his Son Jesus, are now the dwelling place of the Almighty, the temple of God himself who lives amongst them by his Spirit. So, Christians affirm both the transcendence and immanence of God.

Modern spirituality is more focused on the human spirit than the divine. The gods of today's spiritual questers are the gods which are found within, more than the God who lives and reigns without. Indeed, the rejection of the God above has led people to pursue the god within. As one art critic expressed it, "When the sky-god expired, the earth gods were reanimated".[39] When people speak of their communion with the spirit in nature, with the life force that energizes all living things, they are reflecting a theology of a God who is imma-nent, not transcendent. The spirit that pervades all living things is also found as one focuses on one's inner being. One New Age web site announces that "The messiah, the liberator, is within us!" (joy2meu.com). Spiritual awareness begins in the soul of a person, which becomes aware of its connected-ness to all that is around it, both physical and metaphysical. Once one is aware of the transcendental nature of one's humanness then one begins the journey inward leading to a discovery of self-awareness.

Whether one searches in any of the accepted religious tradi-tions, or in modern alternative spiritualities, the call is to go within to explore and discover spiritual truth and wellbeing. Later we will examine the enormous appeal today of medieval mystical practices of spirituality. In most cases they do not direct the seeker to the study of a book or sacred writing, and even less to the teachings of a guide or mentor. Through silence, prayer, and meditation, seekers are directed inwards to where the divine Spirit is found in communion with the human spirit.

Conclusions

It will be clear that these features of the new spirituality are far from being separate and unconnected. A desire for a relation-ship, say with God, goes hand in hand with a longing for that relationship to be real and, to some degree, tangible. Similarly, it is a relationship that touches and impacts all of life.

One observer of the charismatic phenomenon of the 1990's, the Toronto Blessing, described it as "quick, easy and consumer-oriented, a sort of McDonaldization of mysticism". He went on to describe it is a bargain freebie in which participants gave up their rationality in return for a warm (some-times romantic or sexual) feeling. It cost nothing in terms of study, work, or prayer, and pilgrims received a reassuring, comforting emotional experience.[40] Here was a popular form of Christian spirituality which focused on the experiential. It was essentially non-rational, and its appeal lay in the promises it offered of spiritual healing and well-being. For this observer, at least, it bore all the hallmarks of the consumer society.

As one examines these features of contemporary spiritu-ality, Christian observers should be struck as much as by what is absent as by what is present. There is little mention of the place of the mind and the critical faculties. The Bible, on the other hand, is clear that while the rational is not the sum total of an encounter with the living God, it is indispensable. Knowing God cannot be divorced from thinking, reasoning, studying, understanding, and grappling with propositional truths. Little is also made of objective truth, the sort of truth that simultaneously establishes the veracity and reliability of some truth claims, while rendering other competing views invalid. Amongst contemporary Christian spiritualities there is little, if anything, of the exclusive claims of Jesus Christ, the God/man who will tolerate no rival claimants. In much of modern spirituality, themes such as sacrifice, suffering, denying oneself, and commitment are, at best, muted, and often entirely absent. There is no mention of costly obedience. The concept that people have been created for God and for his glory is largely absent. As Paul reflects on the many spiritual blessings he enjoys in Jesus Christ, the continual refrain of the passage is that we might live to the praise of Christ's glory (Eph 3). The God of glory and unapproachable holiness, has become the divine vending machine, dispensing blessings at the drop of a prayer or the swipe of a credit card.

We have seen that while people might popularly associate 'the new spirituality' with those particular religious expressions known collectively as 'the New Age', it really is a wider social phenomenon. It reflects trends that have been developing in Western society for almost a generation. It is not surprising, then, that we should find characteristics of 'the new spirituality' in all kinds of religious expression, from the Zen Buddhist to the occult, and even to the conservative Christian evangelical.

There are certainly historical and sociological reasons for the remarkable interest in spirituality in our society. But is that all we can say? Are we simply the victims of powerful social trends? Is there not something intrinsic to us as human beings created in the image of God which can account for the contemporary fascination with spirituality? In other words, isn't there a theological perspective on what is happening around us? It is to an analysis of the true character of the searchings of spiritual seekers that we now turn.

ENDNOTES

1   *Sunday Telegraph*, 2nd September, 2001.

2   David Tacey, *ReEnchantment: The New Australian Spirituality*, HarperCollins, Sydney, 2000, pp. 45-46.

3   DB Knox, *Selected Works Volume I: The Doctrine of God*, Matthias Media, Sydney, 2000, p. 75.

4   Tacey, *ReEnchantment*, p. 17.

5   Jeffrey G Sobosan, *Bless the Beasts: A Spirituality of Animal Care*, Crossroad, New York, 1991, p. 144.

6   Jung, *We are Home*, p. 40.

7   Tacey, *The Spirituality Revolution*, p. 186.

8   Roof, *Spiritual Marketplace*, p. 163.

9   *The Sydney Morning Herald*, Saturday 14th July, 2001.

10 Blanca Greenberg, 'The essence of spirituality', www.religionquest.com.

11 Bruce Demarest, *Satisfy Your Soul: Restoring the Heart of Christian Spirituality*, NavPress, Colorado Springs, 1999, p. 17.

12 Russell Spittler, 'Implicit values in pentecostal missions', *Missiology*, 1988, XVI, p. 412.

13 Daniel E Albrecht, *Rites in the Spirit: A Ritual Approach to Pentecostal/ Charismatic Spirituality*, Academic Press, Sheffield, 1999, p. 226.

14 Tacey, *Re-enchantment*, p. 198.

15 John Shea, *Spirituality and Health Care: Reaching Toward a Holistic Future*, The Park Ridge Centre, Chicago, 2000, pp. 5-6.

16 Tacey, *The Spirituality Revolution*, p. 164.

17 Kathleen Norris, *The Cloister Walk*, Lion, Oxford, 1996, p. 14.

18 www.joy2meu.com/Metaphysical.html.

19 Louise L Hay et al, *Today's Wisdom*, Nacson & Sons, Sydney, 2001, p. 15.

20 Quoted by Gary Collins, *The Soul Search*, p. 35.

21 Wuthnow, *After Heaven*, p. 121.

22 Wuthnow, *After Heaven*, p. 132.

23 Kimon Sargeant, *Seeker Churches: Promoting Traditional Religion in a Non-Traditional Way*, Rutgers University Press, New Brunswick, NJ, 2000, p. 83.

24 Sargeant, *Seeker Churches*, p. 104.

25 Quoted by Greg Pritchard, *The Willow Creek Seeker Service*, Baker, Grand Rapids, 1996, p. 236.

26 Burney, www.joy2meu.com/Atheists.html.

27 Sargeant, *Seeker Services*, p. 99.

28 John Shea, *Spirituality and Health Care*, pp. 98-99.

29 Tacey, *The Spirituality Revolution*, p. 147.

30 Shea, *Spirituality and Health Care*, p. 30.

31 David Wells, *God in the Wasteland: The Reality of Truth in a World of Fading Dreams*, Eerdmans, Grand Rapids, 1994, p. 67.

32 Shea, *Spirituality and Health Care*, p. 27.

33 Sargeant, *Seeker Services*, p. 20.

34 Warren, *The Purpose Driven Church*, Zondervan, Grand Rapids, 1995, p. 198.

35 Quoted by Pritchard, *Willow Creek Seeker Services*, p. 245.

36 Wells, *God in the Wasteland*, p. 115.

37 Brian Houston, *You Need More Money: Discovering God's Amazing Financial Plan for Your Life*, Maximised Leadership Inc., Castle Hill, 1999, p. 13.

38 Houston, *You Need More Money*, p. 97.

39 Peter Conrad, quoted by David Tacey, *Re-enchantment,* p. 108.
40 Nigel Scotland, 'Shopping for a Church', in Craig Bartholomew and
    Thorsten Moritz (eds), *Christ and Consumerism: A Critical Analysis of the
    Spirit of the Age*, Paternoster, Carlisle, 2000 p. 142.

Chapter 5

Spiritual
Seekers?

WE HAVE LOOKED briefly at the spirituality phenomenon as it expresses itself in our society. We have seen that, broadly understood, the new spirituality is presented as the desire of the human spirit for connection with the Other, or the divine. Much of spirituality, be it Christian or non-Christian, is concerned with the care or nurture of the human soul or spirit.

Underlying so much thinking today about spirituality, and even the responses of Christians to this phenomenon, is the assumption that people are 'spiritual seekers'. This is an assumption that we cannot leave unquestioned or unexamined. Is that how the Bible views people outside of Christ? Is the fascination with alternative spiritualities really an expression of peoples' longing for God? Do events like the Mind Body Spirit Festival display the attempts of people to reach out for the God they know is there in the hope that they will truly connect with him? To what extent is the new spirituality truly spiritual, in the sense that it is an expression of the work of the Spirit of God in people's lives? In other words, what is the Bible's perspective on the current spirituality explosion?

The apostle Paul's spiritual smorgasbord

Firstly, how should we understand and respond to this increased awareness in people around us of the spiritual dimension? An obvious point to make is that it should neither surprise us nor alarm us. For years Christians have been preaching that secular materialism is a false god. They have been warning that the pursuit of pleasure, satisfaction, and meaning in life via the accumulation of wealth and possessions is ultimately a frustrating and barren endeavour.

Today, in the wake of the rampant consumerism which was

let loose in the 1960s and 1970s, many people are discovering this fact to be true in their experience. They have it all (or, at least, plenty of it) and are still missing something central and essential. In a sense, therefore, the spirituality explosion only bears out the accuracy of the Christian's diagnosis of the human condition. We told you so.

However, is that all we can say? Does the Bible help us to understand the spiritual cravings of people? We know that Paul, for example, lived in a world of many different kinds of spiritualities (to use the modern term). Like many cities today, the Mediterranean world of the first-century played host to a wide variety of religions and cults. There was the officially sanctioned imperial cult, and the sanctuaries to the widely worshipped gods of Neptune, Apollo and Artemis. Throughout the empire there were various expressions of the worship of the gods of the Egyptians, Isis and Serapis. Mystery cults abounded in the Mediterranean world. There was a cult relating to Black Aphrodite, who only came out at night, the healing god Asklepios, the mother goddess Cybele, the goddess Atergatis and her male consort, Hadad. Further, sacred rocks and mountains were objects of worship. Apart from all this, virtually every city and people had their own patron deities and these were by no means all of Greek or Roman origin.[1]

Given that this was the world in which Paul travelled and preached, it is not surprising that he commented on the religious behaviour of people that he observed everywhere he went. The most penetrating analysis we have of people's religious activities and the motives that underlie them is found in the opening chapter of Paul's epistle to the Romans. What Paul writes here is absolutely foundational for our understanding of people as 'spiritual beings', and the ways in which they express their spiritual longings.

The Romans diagnosis

When you meet people of faiths or spiritualities other than your own you are often struck by their evident sincerity. They genuinely believe in what they are practising. You may consider them to be wrong or deluded, but their innate sincerity seems to be beyond question.

Of course, discerning the motivations and attitudes of the human heart is a very risky business; indeed, it is virtually impossible. The writer of Proverbs observes, "All the ways of a man are pure in his own eyes, but the Lord weighs the spirit" (16:2). Even if we are honest, we often can't be sure of our own motives. As far as we can tell they are pure, but we know how complex and fragile we are as people and therefore we know that there might be a whole range of reasons why we choose a certain course of action. There is only one who rightly and accurately discerns the motives of the human heart, and we must turn to his diagnosis of the human condition.

1. The indictment: truth suppressors v.18

In Romans 1 Paul begins his explanation of the gospel of which he is not ashamed. It is the revelation of God's right-eousness (1:16-17). God's eternal plan and purpose to save his people is now being revealed as the Lord Jesus Christ is proclaimed and believed upon throughout the world.

But it is not just the righteousness of God which is being continually revealed. Paul also says that concurrently we see the daily, ongoing revelation of the wrath of God. We tend to associate God's wrath with the final judgement; that terrifying last day when all the wicked will feel the unbearable blast of his righteous fury and indignation. But for Paul this final day of wrath is just the climax and culmination of what God has been doing on a daily basis ever since the fall of man. As you wake up every day, and assuming you have eyes to see, you can witness both the revelation of God's righteousness in the preaching of the gospel and the saving of people, and all around you the expression of God's wrath and judgement.

Paul goes on to assert that this wrath is "against all ungodliness and unrighteousness of men, who by their unrighteousness suppress the truth" (1:18). This truth, as Paul goes on to say, is the truth about God. This is Paul's indictment of all people, and it is a devastating indictment: they have suppressed the truth. It is almost as if the truth is a dynamic, a power that if it could be let loose would produce enormous good. It would set people free to do righteousness. Yet people in their wickedness suppress or restrain or hold the truth back.

From mid-2002 until the end of the war against Iraq in April 2003, that nation and its conflict with a small coalition of Western nations dominated the world headlines. There were accusations and counter-accusations about Iraq's weapons of mass destruction. As ordinary members of the public, it was virtually impossible for us to know the truth about Iraq. But let us suppose, for argument's sake, that the weapons inspectors had conclusive evidence that Iraq did not have any nuclear, biological or chemical weapons. They then wrote a report to that effect and gave it to members of the UN Security Council, who then deliberately suppressed it. They put the report in a vault and refused to acknowledge its existence. And then to fulfil their own wicked intentions and ambitions, they went to war as if such a truth had never been discovered. That would be an awful thing to do. Yet, that is the kind of picture that Paul paints here. This, says Paul, is what people are doing with the truth about God. They know the truth, but because of sheer wickedness, decide to bury this truth and keep on living as if it never existed.

2. The compelling proof

Paul then presents the proof to support this indictment:

> For what can be known about God is plain to them, because God has shown it to them. For his invisible attributes, namely, his eternal power and divine nature, have been clearly perceived, ever since the creation of the world, in the things that have been made (1:19-20).

Sometimes evangelical Christians, who rightly emphasize the centrality of the Bible, can underplay the significance and importance of creation as a testimony to God. We should be students of the world as well as the word, and both should evoke in us a response of faith, humility, and praise.

Traditionally, Christians have thought that God has authored two books: the book of creation, and the book of scripture. They are not in conflict with each other. Indeed, they cannot be because they both have the one author, and so both must proclaim the one truth. Paul then makes the point that both books speak with clarity. To those whose eyes have been opened, both books reveal the truth about God. But those with darkened minds twist both books, distort the message they proclaim, and suppress the revelation they bring.

Certainly, scripture is a fuller, more complete revelation, and there is so much about God, his character, and his saving purposes that we could never deduce from the things he has created. For example, I don't think for a moment you could look at a three-leaf shamrock and deduce that God is trinity! At the same time we must not minimize the clarity of creation. Paul says that the truth about God is manifest. It is made known because God has made it known. Paul presents us here with a powerful oxymoron (an expression which seems a contradiction in terms, like 'dry rain'). Paul writes that the *aorata*, the invisible things, are *kathoratai*, clearly visible. The hidden is manifest. The unseen is there for all to see! And this knowledge has been made known from the time the world was created.

The amazing beauty and intricacy of each and every part of the creation is breathtaking. An honest appraisal of creation must lead one to conclude that behind this world stands a being of stupendous power and wisdom. And if that is the case, then the creation doesn't just tell me something about God, but also something important about myself and how I must respond to him. I am just a creature, but a creature of such worth that this God would go to remarkable lengths to feed and sustain me. He sends the rain and the sunshine to bring life to crops and animals that nourish me. He sends the light so that I can work, and then the darkness so that I can rest. I must realize that everything I have is a gift from God, and I am simply the recipient. These facts, says Paul, are as plain as the nose on your face, and in the light of them the only right, just, and decent thing to do is to honour God as God and give him thanks.

In summary, Paul's point is that God has made himself perfectly clear, and if there is unbelief in the world then the blame is not to be laid at the feet of God and his revelation.

The blame lies fully and squarely at the feet of sinful people who have suppressed the truth.

Not surprisingly, it is not just Christian apologists who have affirmed these truths. Honest unbelievers, in moments of great candidness, have also acknowledged this. In his book *Long Journey Home*, Os Guinness presents a catalogue of confessions by prominent unbelievers, all bearing out the sober diagnosis of Paul in Romans 1. The French filmmaker Francois Truffaut, for instance, admitted, "There is in me a refusal to learn that is as powerful as my desire to know." Aldous Huxley, in his public confessional *Ends and Means*, admitted that he "took it for granted" that the world had no meaning. He then went on to admit, "I had motives for not wanting the world to have meaning. Consequently I assumed that it had none, and was able without difficulty to find satisfying reason for this assumption". Huxley admitted that he reached this view for "non-intellectual reasons". Huxley then went even further: "It is our will then that decides how and upon what subject we shall use our intelligence". After all, he continued,

> the philosopher who finds no meaning in the world is not concerned exclusively with a problem in metaphysics. He is also concerned to prove that there is no valid reason why he personally should not do as he wants, or why his friends should not seize political power and govern in the way they find most advantageous to themselves.

Guinness rightly notes that Huxley's irrationality is blatant. Huxley readily admits that his beliefs and commitments are self-serving. His own conclusion is damning:

For myself, no doubt as for most of my contemporaries, the philosophy of meaninglessness was essentially liberation from a certain political and economic system and liberation from a certain system of morality. We objected to the morality because it interfered with our sexual freedom.

In layman's words, he admits that we believed in what we wanted to believe in because it set us free to do what we wanted to do. Guinness rightly notes that these and other comments from human experience underline the Bible's analysis that fallen human beings are essentially truth twisters.[2]

3. The verdict

Therefore, Paul draws the only conclusion one can draw from the evidence: "so they are without excuse" (1:20). The term suggests that from a legal standpoint people have been stripped of any defence. In the heavenly Supreme Court, as the guilty offender is presented with the overwhelming case against him or her, then they are left without a word of excuse to offer.

Evangelicals have tended to let people off too lightly. We have so much put the stress on how *little* can be known about God through what is called general or natural revelation, that we have forgotten how much *can* be known. Paul's indictment here is not that people are without knowledge, but that they are without excuse.

4. The great exchange

In the next few verses of Romans 1, Paul develops his argument. In verses 18-20, the focus was on God and his self-revelation, and how God has manifestly made clear to everyone his existence. In the next verses, 21-23, the focus is on the response of people to this self-revelation. He has already told us that they've suppressed the truth about God, but how does this suppression work itself out in people's lives? Listen to what Paul says.

"For although they knew God ... " (v. 21a).
People know God. In the light of what Paul has just said, the knowledge people have of God is that knowledge which can be perceived from the things he has created. It is a cognitive knowledge, not a relational knowledge. Very often when the Bible speaks of knowing God it implies a relational experience of this God, analogous to a man 'knowing' his wife. But in the context, this cannot be the sort of knowledge Paul is speaking about on this occasion. What people know is God's eternal power and divine nature. This tells us that, whatever else we might want to say about people with respect to their spirituality, we can certainly affirm that people know God, and recognize that they have a moral obligation to respond appropriately to that God.

Certainly, the knowledge people have about God from the created order may be limited, but it is sufficient to warrant from every person a twofold response: to glorify God and give him thanks.

Naturally, the more we know of God and his great saving acts, chiefly expressed in the incarnation, crucifixion, resurrection and ascension of the Lord Jesus, then there is all the more reason for a deeper expression of glory and honour. Nevertheless, if the sum total of the knowledge people have of God is that which can be gleaned from creation, then that would be sufficient and render every person morally culpable for not giving God the glory and gratitude he deserves. Bart Simpson's infamous 'grace' before the evening meal, "Dear God, we paid for all this ourselves, so thanks for nothing", puts it more bluntly than most people would dare, but his irreverence captures something of what Paul is saying here.

The psalmist tells us that "the heavens declare the glory of God, and the sky above proclaims his handiwork. *Day to day pours out speech, and night to night reveals knowledge"* (19:1-2). There is a daily sermon from creation and people are held responsible before God if they close their ears and eyes to what is being said.

Trading in the truth
Having highlighted what wicked people have not done in failing to glorify God, Paul now describes what they have done. In three virtually parallel expressions he describes the active, culpable wickedness and unbelief of people.

Firstly, they became futile or empty in their reasoning about God, and their senseless minds were darkened (v. 21c). In other words, their natural capacity to reason accurately about God is profoundly damaged. There is a darkness or spiritual callousness at the core of each human being which makes it impossible for them to perceive spiritual truth.

I was talking recently to a young Chinese woman, who is a very keen Christian. I asked her about her family, and she said that it wasn't easy for her because both of her parents were atheists. They saw themselves as rational, committed atheists. Then she went on to say that despite this ideological commitment, in times of crisis, for example when one of their children is about to sit an exam or has a job interview, then they have a little shrine in their apartment and they light incense and say prayers. "And they're atheists?" I said to her. "That's right", she said, "they don't believe God exists". The logical inconsistency is staggering. Offering prayers to a being or beings you don't believe exist!

Secondly, Paul expresses this same truth in another way, by pointing out the disjunction between what they profess about themselves and what they actually demonstrate. The disjunction is between the pretension and the reality: "claiming to be wise, they became fools". People claim to have experienced and reasoned out the truth about spirituality and the meaning of life. Bookshops and websites are full of their publications. Yet, says Paul, when you see how this wisdom practically expresses itself, then you come face to face with folly. There is something tragic and pathetic about human beings feeling that a bird is *actually* their brother, or a rock is their friend. Similarly, it is sad that people are duped into thinking that true wellbeing and happiness is found in travelling with a spirit guide, or meeting an angel, or following some 12-step formula for spiritual wholeness.

Thirdly, This folly is nowhere more poignantly expressed than in people's desire to exchange "the glory of the immortal God for images resembling mortal man, and birds, and animals and reptiles" (v. 23). It is quite likely that Paul has in his mind here Psalm 106:

They made a calf in Horeb
and worshipped a metal image.
They exchanged the glory of God
for the image of an ox that eats grass.
They forgot God, their Saviour,
who had done great things in Egypt,

> wondrous works in the land of Ham,
> and awesome deeds by the Red Sea. (vv. 19-22)

The psalmist says that, spiritually, Israel has exchanged a delicious *a la carte* lunch for a meat pie. For Israel, the God of creation was their God. He was their Glory. They knew and experienced his majesty, and they basked in the wonder of knowing him. Yet they surrendered all of this for an idol. They traded in their Glory for pieces of metal and for lumps of wood.

And Paul says that this is what all people do. Whether they are reading the tarot cards down at the Mind Body Spirit Festival, or following one of the countless gods of the Hindu religion, or listening to the latest messiah from the newest cult out of Southern California. At every corner we see the evidence that people have a knowledge of God. We can testify to the gropings of people who are expressing their innate awareness of a Being who orders and rules their world. Yet, at the same time, these very religious activities are an expression of that essential wickedness and rebellion which is the essence of human sin.

The Romans diagnosis and the new spirituality

As we live in a society of so many competing spiritualities we desperately need to hear Paul's words on the human condition. We need to listen to God's diagnosis of the real character of people's spiritual motivations. We can be tempted to look at the new spirituality and people's hunger for 'spiritual connection', and see it as the genuine longing of sincere spiritual seekers. We may point to the New Age movement, or the

contemporary fascination with Eastern religions, or the rediscovery of ancient spiritualities, and think that they are all
pointers to the fact that people are essentially spiritual seekers.
People are looking for God and longing to get in contact with
the One they know is there. Then we might conclude that trag-
ically they are looking in the wrong place, and if only there
were someone who could point them in the right direction,
then, like the prodigal son, they would hurry home.

There is, of course, an element of truth in all that. The
phenomenal growth of the new spirituality does point to
people's awareness of the presence of God. But, says Paul,
such movements are not the signposts of spiritual seekers.
They are, in reality, the hallmarks of spiritual hiders, of religious runaways, of divine deniers.

The Mind Body Spirit Festival is much more than a testimony to spiritual hunger. It is a festival of human wickedness.
Here we see on a large scale that people have taken the glory
of the incorruptible God, and exchanged it for the stars in the
sky, or the lines on the palm of your hand, or the darkened
wisdom of the latest guru or clairvoyant.

When you read modern Christian books on comparative
religions, or analyses of the religious condition of people, it is
remarkable that Romans 1 is rarely mentioned. Yet, as we have
seen, it presents us with the most fundamental diagnosis of
the character of people's religious behaviour.

Certainly, people long for wholeness and wellbeing. But the
fact that they end up anywhere except humbly on their knees
before this God tells us something about their true motivations.
God knows the hearts of all people, and in Romans 1, through
his servant Paul, he presents us with a very different verdict on
alternative spiritualities, whether ancient or modern.

The spirit and the spiritualities

Both the term 'spirituality' itself, and the fact that so many people testify to spiritual experiences, demands the question: is this resurgence of an interest in the things of the spirit actually a sign of the working of the Holy Spirit in people's lives? When a rock climber's senses are stimulated by a sense of the holy leading to an attitude of reverence and trust in the rock on which he is clinging, are these the promptings of the Spirit of God? In short, how truly spiritual is spirituality?

It seems helpful to distinguish 'spirit' from 'Spirit'. We have already noted that contemporary spirituality is inner focussed, dwelling on the aspirations and sensations of the human spirit. The question being raised here, then, is what is the relationship between the human spirit and the Holy Spirit? A second and closely related question is, to what extent does the Spirit of God work in the world? Is he at work in the hearts of those of other faiths? Can his presence be discerned in those movements for peace and social improvement across the globe? For example, is the Holy Spirit behind the Middle East Peace process, or efforts at humanitarian aid when an earthquake devastates a country, even when those participating in such activities are not professing Christians?

The difficulty we have in answering these sorts of questions is that it seems to be a topic that the scriptures do not directly address. It is clear that all men and women are spiritual in the sense that there is in each person a human spirit. Indeed, in its most general sense one can speak of all animate beings having a spirit, understood as that which gives them life (Eccl 3:19-21, Luke 8:55). When the New Testament speaks of the human spirit it is referring to men and women in so far as they belong to, and interact with, the spiritual realm.

However, while scripture and human experience testify to people's self-awareness of this spiritual realm, it is striking that the Bible does not speak of this in the context of the work of the Holy Spirit. The writers of the Bible do not speak of this spirit as some 'divine spark' inhabiting the body. To the contrary, for inspired observers of the human condition like Paul, men and women outside of Christ are spiritually dead, "having no hope and without God in the world" (Eph 2:12).

Further, while it is common today to speak of the cosmic spirit who is at work in the hearts of people, such a theology runs counter to the New Testament. In fact, Jesus placed the Spirit and the world in an antithetical relationship, saying, "the Spirit of truth, whom the world cannot receive, because it neither sees him nor knows him" (John 14:17). The Spirit convicts the world of sin, righteousness and judgement (John 16:8-11).

When one turns to what the New Testament has to say about the relationship of the Holy Spirit to the unbelieving world, the silence is deafening. Strikingly, in Gordon Fee's mammoth 1000-page analysis of the Spirit in the writings of Paul, *God's Empowering Presence*, there is not a single reference to the Spirit's relationship to the world. This is not a testimony to the inadequacy of Fee's treatment, but to the fact that Paul sees no such relationship. The conclusion of Griffith Thomas made early last century is remarkably apt:

> Although most modern writers on the subject of the Holy Spirit speak of the Spirit as related to the world of mankind, nothing is more striking than the simple fact that not a single passage can be discovered in the New Testament which refers to the direct action of the Spirit on the world.[3]

In summary, then, we have seen that the Bible says that all people have a 'spirit', which infuses them and gives them life. We have also seen from Romans 1 that people have a knowledge of God, and they express that awareness in acts of religious or spiritual devotion. At the same time the natural, fallen person cannot understand spiritual truth. Indeed, the curse of the fall remains, that "my Spirit shall not abide in man forever, for he is flesh" (Gen 6:3). If we use the term 'spiritual' to describe one aspect of men and women (along with the fact that we are physical, emotional, and so forth), then we need to understand that, biblically understood, this concept cannot be taken to suggest that all people are indwelt by the Spirit of the living God. Rather, we are simply asserting that there is a dimension of their personality which has an awareness of God, but that this understanding has been corrupted by sin.

What of God's Spirit at work in the world? We've noted the silence of the scriptures on this issue, yet at the same time we certainly want to affirm that God, by his Spirit, is involved with the world he created and sustains. God can, and does, work through all sorts of people to achieve his good purposes. The Persian king, Cyrus (6th century BC), is a case in point. In order to bring about the rebuilding of the Temple, the writer of 2 Chronicles comments, "[so] that the word of the LORD by the mouth of Jeremiah might be fulfilled, the Lord stirred up the spirit of Cyrus king of Persia, so that he made a proclamation throughout all his kingdom" (2 Chron 36:22). Here is a pagan ruler, whom nevertheless God makes sympathetic to the plight of God's people. We can speak of God, by his Spirit, moving people's hearts to achieve his good purposes. It is for this reason that we can thank God for new medical discoveries, movements towards world peace, and famine relief—as well as giving honour to those men and women through whom he has worked to achieve these ends.

Calvin helpfully distinguished between the general and saving activities of the Spirit. He writes that God's Spirit assists men and women in physics, dialectic, mathematics and other disciplines. Similarly, one can rightly see works of peace and charity in the world as marks of the mercy of God by his Spirit. But the ultimate purpose of such kindnesses is to bring people to repentance and faith. This is accomplished by the Spirit in the lives of those who put their faith in Christ. In short, it is one thing to see, and affirm, God's Spirit working through all sorts of people to achieve God's good purposes for his creation. However, this is distinct from God's Spirit living in people, bringing to them saving knowledge, and making them part of the kingdom of his Son, the Lord Jesus.

> In attributing all good to the Spirit's activity, we must be careful to underline that the Spirit dwells in believers only. Not all divine activity is saving activity.[4]

The Spirit is the Spirit of Jesus and therefore, fundamentally, every experience of the Holy Spirit can be evaluated in terms of the place it gives to the Lord Jesus Christ. That which glorifies him is truly spiritual. That which does not do so the New Testament does not attribute to the saving work of the Holy Spirit.

Speaking in the spiritual marketplace—lessons from the apostle Paul

One of the best commentaries on the current spirituality craze comes from the rather cynical and pessimistic Teacher of

Ecclesiastes who writes of God that "he has put eternity into man's heart, yet so that he cannot find out what God has done from the beginning to the end" (3:11). This is really what we have seen Paul affirm in Romans 1. God has given to people an awareness that there is more to life than just the physical. There is a knowledge of God and, therefore, an awareness of a dimension to human existence which transcends the physical and material. That is why people have always spoken of their 'spiritual yearnings'. People know that there is more to life than what can be touched, seen, heard and felt. This is the deliberate work of God, who has put this sense of the transcendent, or the eternal, in their hearts.

However, the Teacher then draws the despairing conclusion from that observation: *yet they cannot find out what God has done from the beginning to the end.* In short, while God has put this divine awareness in people's hearts, there is wrapped around this sense of the eternal a veil, so that while people reach out for the transcendent they constantly get wrong the character of its essential reality, or how to appropriately respond to it.

Paul preaches Romans 1

What the Teacher of Ecclesiastes observed in his day, and what Paul was to write to the Christians in Rome, was what he observed as he travelled around the Roman world. Acts 17 recounts Paul's visit to Athens, the cultural centre of the world, and the speech which he delivered to the people of that city in the Areopagus, the city's chief court. Here we see Paul taking his theology and preaching it. Here Paul comes face to face with the sort of people whose suppression of the truth he is later to write about. How does he address them? Is he unyielding and confrontational? Does he tone down his blunt language of Romans in the face of real, sincere worshippers who may be potential converts? How does Paul preach Romans 1?

Paul's address is often presented as a model of a sensitive and sympathetic interaction with believers from other faith traditions. For example, Ken Gnanakan writes of "Paul's attempts to establish a continuity between the gospel and the worship of the Athenians", and "Paul was able to commend Athenian worship".[5] This would be very odd given what we have just seen Paul write to the Romans about idolaters like the Athenians. Of course, it's possible Paul took a harder line about idolatry later in his ministry. Given the mixed reception his speech to the Athenians received, some have postulated that Paul decided it was time for a change of strategy. Perhaps he was annoyed that they weren't more sympathetic to his concil-iatory 'softly softly' approach to evangelism, and later became much more uncompromising in his denunciation of false worship. While it is not uncommon for people to change or moderate their viewpoint, we'll see that there is absolutely no need to resort to such a fanciful reconstruction when it comes to Paul's address in Athens. In fact, what we read about in Acts 17 is Paul putting into an address the very same assertions that he was to put down on paper to the Christians in Rome. The perceptive reader will find Paul's devastating critique of false worship in Romans 1 clearly echoed as he exposes the foolish-ness and emptiness of Athenian religious practices.

While waiting for his friends and fellow travellers, Silas and Timothy, Paul finds himself in the middle of a vast array of idols, statues, shrines and temples. In a little while the apostle will be given an opportunity to speak before the Athenian council on Mars Hill, but before he does, his narrator, Luke, gives us an insight into what was going on in Paul's heart as he found himself in the middle of a veritable forest of idols. Luke records that "his spirit was provoked within him as he saw that the city was full of idols" (v. 16). The word which is translated "provoked" is a strong verb (from which we derive our modern word 'paroxysm'), and it is usually used in contexts where it means to stir up sharp emotions. Paul is feeling intense emotional revulsion. He had seen idolatry before, but never on the scale that he witnessed that day, and it has made him sick to the stomach.

With his stomach churning, Paul stands to preach. Here is Paul in an ancient equivalent to the Mind Body Spirit Festival. What does he say?

Paul opens his address by describing the Athenians as "extremely religious" (v. 22). The actual word Paul used (*deisidaimonesterous*) is an ambiguous term which can be interpreted either positively or pejoratively. It can mean "very religious", and it is quite correct to translate it this way, but it can also mean "extremely superstitious". Which one does Paul mean? Is Paul rather impressed by how spiritual the Athenians are, or is he aghast at the breadth and depth of such superstitious nonsense? Does he find their unrestrained idolatry admirable or abhorrent? In describing Paul's visceral response to Athenian idolatry Luke has already given us the answer to these questions.

When Paul was brought before the council which met on Mars Hill he wasn't strictly on trial, but these were the men who regulated the religious life of the city, and complaints had been levelled against Paul. Some had accused him of proclaiming new, and presumably unauthorized, foreign gods (Acts 17:18). In other words, here is a context in which Paul would have to choose his words carefully. Therefore, he is hardly going to begin his defence by insulting the very men before whom he has been called to give an account. So, there is little doubt that they would have understood Paul's words more positively. On the other hand, we know what Paul really thinks of their spirituality: he's been revolted and disgusted by it. So, for the discerning listener, there can similarly be little doubt as to what Paul really meant by the word.

But Paul has chosen this word very carefully. Indeed, throughout the entire speech Paul makes use of what is known as the *double entendre:* words which in the hearers' ears may have one meaning, to the astute and discerning listener mean something completely different altogether.[6] On one level, the Athenians may find little to object to in Paul's address; he has acknowledged their religiosity and will appear to continue in the same cordial tone. However, we who have been told what Paul really thinks of their idolatry will understand the address as a devastating critique of the ignorance and foolishness of all religious idolatry.

Ignorant knowledge

Paul then gives support for his contention that the Athenians are very religious. Amongst the smorgasbord of idols he has seen another one, and it bears the ascription, *to the unknown god.*

Some of the Athenians may have assumed that Paul was recognising the breadth of their religious knowledge, and that he just wanted to extend their circle of understanding a little wider by filling in the details about this unknown god.

However, Luke has already given sufficient indications of the apostle's attitude towards the religion of the Athenians. He has felt the same deep revulsion that gripped the ancient prophets of Yahweh. Even this 'unknown god' is itself an idol. We cannot be sure what Paul actually saw, but it was some sort of statue, perhaps of a man. The inscription did not bear witness to the fact that some in that city had experiential knowledge of the true and living God and were only waiting for someone to come to them and reveal to them his name and the complete details of his character. These are not the pagan equivalents to the Ethiopian eunuch in Acts 8, reading Isaiah, and just waiting for an interpreter to come alongside them.

To the contrary, this idol was a very public testimony to their almost total ignorance regarding the truth about God. In the midst of the smorgasbord of gods, there is an acknowledgment by some of the existence of another god, but at the same time an admission of the fact that they are not able to make any meaningful statement about this god, apart from the fact that he exists. In other words, here in the midst of Athens is an idol and its name is 'Ignorance', or 'I don't know'! This is precisely the thing that we saw Paul affirm about men and women in Romans 1. Clearly, these people are not worshipping God. Paul is really saying that the most knowledgeable of the Athenians have reached the point where they now know how little they actually know!

The apostle then goes on to point out the absurdity of thinking that the God of heaven and earth can be confined into a temple, or that the God who made everything, and gives us the very breath we need to stay alive is somehow dependent on things that we give him (vv. 24-25). I remember years ago sitting in my church and I turned and looked at one of the plaques on the wall. You know the ones, 'In memory of so-and-so who died during a particularly long sermon in this church, on the 14th April, 1897', and then a verse. The verse at the bottom of this plaque read, "For the Lord hath need of him" (Luke 19:31). I found that a strange and startling verse. I was sure I'd been told that God didn't *need* anyone or anything. Wasn't that the very point that Paul was making to the Athenians? Did Paul get it wrong? I looked up Luke 19:31. It is the passage describing Jesus' entry into Jerusalem. He instructs two of his disciples,

> Go into the village in front of you, where on entering you will find a colt tied ... untie it and bring it here. If anyone asks you, 'Why are you untying it?' you shall say this: '*The Lord has need of it.*'

Older versions rendered the word 'colt' as 'donkey' or 'ass'. It struck me that this was not a particularly endearing way to refer to a deceased relative: an ass. Although, of course, it wasn't the dearly departed who was the ass, but the donkey who chose this inscription.

To think the Lord, who made all things, needs you or anything you have to offer would make you a donkey. And that is the point Paul is making before the Areopagus.

Near ... and yet, so far

Paul goes on to affirm the essential unity of mankind, pointing out that God has made all the nations upon earth from one man, and he has done this with a two-fold purpose: that they may dwell upon earth and that they may seek him (v. 27). Although he is speaking to pagans, the verb 'seek' here probably carries the force of its biblical meaning of 'entering into a relationship with'. So, Paul acknowledges that God has created men and women so that they might know him and relate to him.

Has this desire of God been fulfilled or thwarted? Once again, Paul's answer is ambiguous. At one level, to his audience Paul is expressing the nearness of God, and people's intuitive awareness of this fact. Even their own pagan religious writings bear witness to this fact (v. 28). Yet, at another level, the apostle characterizes the pagans' search for God as a 'groping'. It is the word one would use for the searching hands of a blind person as they stumble around in the darkness. The picture it conjures up is of a seeker frantically and hopelessly searching with arms outstretched, trying desperately to see through the impenetrable haze and take hold of the thing that they know is right there, right before his or her eyes, if only someone would shine some light.

Once again, this is what Paul sees all around him in the spiritual marketplace of ancient Athens. There is evidence, on the one hand, that people know God is there, and not far away. Yet the presence of all these idols just shows that they are groping like blind people in a tragic and futile attempt to lay hold of him.

New Testament commentator Ben Witherington comments on this verse:

> The overall effect of this verse is to highlight the dilemma and irony of the human situation. Though God is omnipresent, and so not far from any person, ironically human beings are stumbling around in the dark trying to find God. When one is blind, even an object right in front of one's face can be missed. The sentence does not encourage us to think the speaker believes that the finding of the true God is actually going on, apart from divine revelation. To the contrary, the true God remains unknown apart from such revelation.[7]

Recapturing the passion—and revulsion—of Paul

The great nineteenth-century missionary to Muslims, Henry Martyn, witnessed at one time in India a Hindu procession. He saw the people prostrating themselves on the ground before things that were little more than stumps of wood, and he said, "this excited in me more horror than I can well express ... I thought that if I had words I would preach to the multitudes all day if I lost my life for it". On another occasion, Martyn wrote, "I could not endure existence if Jesus was not glorified; it would be hell to me, if he were always to be dishonoured". For the apostle Paul to walk amongst the forest of idols in Athens excited within him the very same emotional and visceral response.

It is a sobering experience to wander around the Mind Body Spirit Festival, or to surf the websites of contemporary spiritualities. We understand why people who intuitively know God and are aware that in him they live and move and have their being, grope and search for spiritual connection. We understand the hunger for relationship and the thirst for experience. Yet in the light of the Bible we also recognize how culpably foolish people are in such strivings and why they consistently ignore what is plain to see, and choose to worship the creature rather than the Creator.

When Paul speaks in his own spiritual marketplace he finds points of contact with the people around him. He directs their attention to one of their own idols. He quotes from their own gurus. He exposes the inconsistencies in their world view. He speaks their language. But how he understands the true character of their religious devotion is informed by the scriptures. He uncompromisingly affirms the uniqueness of the Lord, and unashamedly calls upon them to turn from their idolatries because God will judge them for their culpable folly.

There is no hint of any commendation of Athenian worship, and no compromise in his identifying its true character. Certainly, Paul is thoughtful and prudent in the terms he uses. He is as wise as a serpent and as innocent as a dove. But he knows full well that he is not speaking to an audience of sympathetic spiritual seekers, but a city of fools who have chosen images like mortal men and beasts instead of the true God they know is near and present. Paul's passion for God's glory, his grasp of God's truth about men and women, and at the same time his deep desire to see people find the One who is the true object of their gropings, has produced this timeless model of a sermon to shoppers in the spiritual marketplace.

This is not an easy diagnosis for us to hear. All around us we are being told that people are genuine spiritual seekers. We are told that it's not Jesus that people disdain and despise, it is Christians. It is not God that people are rejecting but the church and its preachy, dogmatic imposition of outdated and fearful descriptions of this God. People may be lost, we are told, but they are not rebellious. People's lives may be in a pigsty, but they sincerely want to come home.

There can be no doubting that Jesus Christ's ambassadors have often proven to be very poor diplomats for their King and Saviour. There is certainly a good deal wrong with the church, as there has always been, and we may have to bear some of the responsibility for the fact that people have failed to clearly see Jesus Christ because we have obscured him behind curtains of insensitivity, hypocrisy and stultifying traditions. However, even when the Christian witness is clear, pure and winsome, there is still the spiritual reality that people have wilfully suppressed the truth about God. The frightening verdict on the spiritual condition of humankind found in John's Gospel remains as true for people today as it has ever been: "And this is the judgement: the light has come into the world, and people loved the darkness rather than the light because their deeds were evil" (3:19).

It is only when we see the spiritual condition of people for what it is that we can recognize why the gospel is the *power* of God for salvation. It doesn't take resurrection power to persuade people to do what they want to do anyway. It doesn't take much persuasion to convince a thirsty person to drink some water. However, to convince proud rebels whose deeds are evil of their sin and their need of a Saviour takes a work of the Spirit of God. That's why the work of salvation, which changes hiders into seekers, can only be the work of God. This is why the gospel is a gospel of grace, and why it is the one message that humbles the proud, and gives God all the glory for making the fool wise and bringing the lost home.

ENDNOTES

1   See David WJ Gill, 'Behind the classical facade: local religions of the Roman Empire', in Andrew D Clarke and Bruce Winter (eds), *One God, One Lord in a World of Religious Pluralism*, Tyndale House, Cambridge, 1991.

2   Os Guinness, *Long Journey Home: A Guide to Your Search for the Meaning of Life*, Waterbrook Press, Colorado Springs, 2002, pp. 200-202.

3   Quoted by Sinclair Ferguson, *The Holy Spirit*, IVP, Leicester, 1996, p. 244.

4   Ferguson, *The Holy Spirit*, p. 248.

5   Ken R Gnanakan, 'Are there disciples of Christ outside the church?', in *No Other Gods Before Me: Evangelicals and the Challenge of World Religions*, Baker, Grand Rapids, 2001, p. 182.

6   See the very perceptive analysis of Acts 17 by Mark D Given, 'Not either/or but both/and in Paul's Areopagus speech', *Biblical Interpretation*, 1995, 3, p. 364.

7   Ben Witherington, *The Acts of the Apostles: A Socio-Rhetorical Commentary*, Eerdmans, Grand Rapids, 1998, p. 529.

Chapter 6

Hearing the Mystics

Introduction

We have seen that the 'spirituality phenomenon' is something that is as much a feature of the modern church as it is society as a whole. Christians and non-Christians alike testify that they are searching for encounters with God which are authentic, tangible and rewarding. Contemporary spirituality is about the questings and stirrings of the human soul or spirit.

When the term 'spirituality' is used by Christians (who, of course, first coined the word), they too, by and large, are referring to the state of the human soul. In much Christian writing, spirituality is concerned with the nurture and care of the human spirit. It is about the cultivation of the inner being. We now want to examine more closely how this phenomenon expresses itself in the church.

According to the Lord Jesus, the great duty of every person is to "love the Lord your God with all your heart, with all your soul, and with all your mind" (Matt 22:37). We are to know and love God with every part our being: intellectual, volitional and emotional. For many evangelicals, it seems that we've been very good at loving God with our minds, but have forgotten that we are more than redeemed brains. Until the advent of computers and PowerPoint presentations, the first image a visitor had of attending many churches was being greeted at the door by an usher distributing three or four books (prayer book, Bible, hymn and song books) plus an assorted collection of newspapers, brochures and newssheets. Here was a worship service for the literate. Sunday morning sermons often seemed little different, in both form and content, from university lectures (except some were slightly shorter, and there was no opportunity to ask questions). The most important personal activity in the Christian life was said to be the daily quiet time of prayer and study, and the most important group activity was the weekly Bible study. For some, all these things have their place, but it seemed that it all added up to being little more than a religion of the mind. Again and again, some Christians began to ask, isn't there something more? Isn't there a way to connect with God which involves every part of our humanity, including our spirits and our emotions?

The frustrations many evangelicals face are due, in part, to something that we all agree is central to our faith. Evangelical Christianity has always been an essentially personal expression of Christian faith. It is about a relationship with a God who is real, alive and wanting to personally engage us. It claims that this God can be personally met and encountered. He is the God who comes to us, regenerates us by his Spirit, and by this same Spirit remains always with us. He is the God who hears and answers prayer. Our great frustration is that, at times, he seems so distant, and we are told that we have to claim his presence and his saving benefits by faith. We long for more than that.

Consequently, evangelicals have been intrigued by, and attracted to, those spiritualities which tell us that there *is* something more. To the 'restless remnant' desperate for a divine encounter, it is suggested that God holds out here and now the satisfaction of that hunger. You need no longer be content with talks that speak of the promise of his presence, for now you can experience the power of his presence.

The charismatic alternative

For many evangelicals, charismatic Christianity has offered just such an alternative. Here is a movement that offers a spontaneous, deeply experiential encounter with God. The silent God now speaks in prophecies and words of knowledge. The hidden God is now seen in the signs he manifests in their midst. The God who is a consuming fire is experienced by the believer as the one whose loving arms enfold them, draws them to his side, and overwhelms them with the power of his love.

What is more, charismatic Christianity breaks down the dividing wall that has kept Christians apart for centuries. It is irrelevant now whether you are Protestant or Catholic, Anglican or pentecostal. While doctrines like justification by faith may still be understood differently, what unites is seen to be greater than what divides. Man-made theologies divide, while Spirit-created experiences unite. The supernatural signs of God's presence are manifest in the lives of all kinds of believers and, it seems, God's Spirit is no respecter of human divisions. God works his works of grace and power in the lives of all his children, irrespective of their particular theology. God blesses faith, not correct doctrine, it is said, and while doctrine is not irrelevant, the central thing is a dynamic experience of the Spirit of God.

There is much about charismatic Christianity which is appealing to this generation. It is an age when we want to break down barriers and be more inclusive. Experiences of the Spirit seem to achieve that. We have seen that the new spirituality, in its various manifestations, is much more about the heart than the head. Indeed, when it comes to the question of how a person knows God or knows Christ, it is often said that Christian history records the struggle of the head against the heart, the intellect against the experience or, even, the Word against the Spirit. The former, which expresses itself in creeds, doctrines, and books of theology, is described as a way of knowing about God. The latter, which is the realm of dreams, visions, audible and inaudible words, and tactile sensations, is a way of knowing God. The world of direct experience of the divine is the world of the charismatics ... and the mystics.

The appeal of mysticism

In July 2001, 450 people gathered in Sydney for the John Main seminar, an ecumenical event celebrating the place of Christian meditation and the tradition of contemplative prayer. The speaker, Rowan Williams, then the Archbishop of Wales (now Archbishop of Canterbury) spoke about the relevance of the fourth-century Desert Fathers for Christian living today. The Desert Fathers were men (and women) who fled their society to live an ascetic life of silent contemplation and spiritual warfare, sometimes in total isolation, sometimes in monastic communities. Here was a large gathering of people to hear a series of lectures on what some may consider to be the more eccentric personalities of Christian history.

This is an indication of the widespread revival of interest in early Christian monasticism and medieval mysticism. In a busy society where words bombard us at every juncture—on billboards, via radios and televisions, from pulpits—many are being attracted to the model of withdrawing to places of solace and stillness for reorientation and reflection. Some are suggesting that the secret to a deeper life of devotion to Christ can be found, not in reading more books, or attending more talks, but in quiet, contemplative listening to God. David Tacey sees a return to mysticism as the only hope for a dying church. He writes,

Religion has to shift from moralism to mysticism, with less emphasis on the God 'out there' and more emphasis on the God within ... with the collapse of belief in the traditional image of God, we have to find God in a new place, and the most convincing place of all will be our own human hearts.[1]

Despite the growing interest in the mystics, or in those forms of devotion that draw from the wellsprings of mysticism, most Christians know very little about them. Without doubt, some of the mystics are amongst the most colourful and fascinating characters in the annals of Christian history. However, more recently the writings of a small number have been rediscovered and now these few are achieving a fame and an attention that they haven't known for centuries. Still, most evangelicals remain largely ignorant of what the mystics believed both about God and how we grow in the knowledge of God. There may simply be the perception that here are some of our spiritual forbears who experienced a relationship with God which was extraordinarily personal, and enjoyed a level of intimacy with God which gave them a joy and serenity which many today long for.

In order to understand this revival of interest in mysticism, we need to look at what it is about them, and their understanding and experience of God, that has led so many to find in them help and inspiration for their own spirituality today. As much as possible we need to let them speak for themselves, so that we can properly understand what mysticism is really all about.

Mysticism and the mystics

The English medieval mystic Margery Kempe (ca. 1373–ca. 1436) testified that she'd lived everyday in constant conversation with Christ, often hearing the music of heaven "so loud and real to me that I would be unable to hear what people were saying unless they raised their voices to me". Margery's experience of the divine was certainly more pronounced than that of many other mystics; nevertheless she typifies the strongly subjective nature of their spirituality. Mysticism emphasizes the inward, subjective, intuitive experience of God. The journey of growth in the knowledge of God is largely a journey inward, into the human soul, which is where God makes his home.

For mystics, God and Christ are persons who are known and experienced first-hand, more than as simply objects of belief. The life of faith is essentially the life of being constantly experientially aware of the presence of God. The heart of faith is union with God, and the goal of the life of faith is deeper, perfect union with the Saviour.

How does someone come to know God, and particularly with this degree of closeness? Mystics affirm the importance of the traditional avenues for the knowledge of God, namely, general revelation (God's self-revelation in the things he has made) and special revelation (in particular, in the scriptures). However, they testify to a third avenue of knowledge, which is the higher and greater way, and which alone brings full union with Christ, and that is the way of direct experience.

Mystics soon begin to sound like 'super Christians', who make mere mortals who haven't enjoyed their deeper experience of God feel like second-class citizens of heaven. In fact, some mystics are explicit about the different degrees of Christian living, ranging from the ordinary, through to the special, and ascending into the perfect. There is a clear distinction between those who merely believe in God, and those know his presence as a daily, dynamic, abiding reality. At the same time, it is argued that such mystical encounters with divine love are available for anyone willing to sit at the feet of these spiritual teachers and learn from them. Writers on mysticism affirm that each person has the capacity to reach the spiritual heights of ecstatic union with God, although God does graciously bless some with an intimacy of experience which is special.

Naturally, mysticism was, and is, a many-varied movement, and mystics have differed as much in their practices and beliefs as they have in their personalities. Some were clearly eccentric, others much more moderate in their approach to the contemplative life. Nevertheless, common themes in the practice of mysticism soon become apparent once one begins to read their writings. In particular, many mystics regularly wrote of 'the mystic way', a threefold path to perfect union with Christ. The first stage was purgation, where the beginner, by penitence and effort, purifies himself from worldly entanglements. Secondly, there is illumination, during which the believer more deeply comprehends the beauty of living in the presence of God. Finally, the mystic grows into a state of union, where death to self is complete and he or she is now fully immersed in the indwelling love of God. This final stage "brings astonishing access of energy and endurance, a power of dealing with persons and events far beyond the self's natural capacities".[2]

The emergence of Christian mysticism

Mystics and mystical experience of the divine have apparently always been part of human experiences. Indeed, every religion has its mystics (for example, the Sufis of Islam). Christian advocates of the mystical way point to the apostle Paul as one of the great models and practitioners of mysticism. Of course, followers of any Christian movement tend to find in Paul their founder and exemplar. For conservative evangelicals the apostle was the first theologian and the quintessential preacher of the word. For charismatics he was the first 'pentecostal', who performed signs and wonders, and planted pneumatic churches spontaneously led by the Spirit. For mystics, though, he is the first great mystic, a man of dreams and visions, for whom the central theological principle was personal union with Christ.

However, the emergence of mysticism as a distinct and definable movement in Christian history took place in the fourth century with the rise of monasticism.[3] In 271AD a young and affluent Egyptian Christian named Antony heard a sermon on Matthew 19:21, in which the Lord Jesus told another young man (not unlike Antony himself) that if he would be perfect he should sell what he possessed and give it to the poor. Antony took this as a personal command, and so began a life of extreme asceticism in which he spent twenty years locked up in an old fortress, subjugating his worldly passions and triumphing over the torments of demons. He emerged from this experience having regained the lost image of God, and able to instruct others. Through a biography on his life by Athanasius, Antony's fame spread and inspired thousands of others to embrace a similar lifestyle. Many became, like Antony, anchorites (from the Greek *anachoreo* = to withdraw), monks who lived as recluses, isolated from other human contact. Others followed the practice of Pachomius (290-346) and became caenobites (from the Greek *koinos* = common and *bios* = life), forming monastic communities.

Antony spent his days in prayer and self-discipline, and Athanasius records that he experienced frequent visions. He was given the ability to know the future, and the power to heal. One can easily see the natural link between a monkish lifestyle and mysticism. The goals of the two intersect. Both are concerned with seeking to transcend the mundane and worldly, and reach a higher state of union with God through prayer and contemplation. Such goals are more easily achieved by those who have forsaken the everyday pursuits of life, in particular daily work and marriage, in favour of a life dedicated to the pursuit of God. It is not surprising, therefore, that through the centuries many of the mystical classics were penned by monks, and often monks who chose a hermit-like existence.

Mysticism in the middle ages

For the next 800 years mysticism was strongly monastic and found its inspiration in the lonely asceticism of the Desert Fathers. Mystics continued to be the heroes of the church. None gained more acclaim and reverence than the 12th century ascetic and mystic, Francis of Assisi.

Shortly afterwards, one of the great ages of mysticism dawned. Thirteenth- and fourteenth-century Europe proved to be a fertile ground for the flowering of mysticism. This period was the climax of three centuries of economic prosperity and expansion in Europe. New agricultural techniques and warmer climates led to population growth, an increase in trade, and urban growth. A literate mercantile class developed, which led to the flowering of literature and, in particular, vernacular translations of the Bible. Now, for the first time, mystical works were being written by people outside the monasteries, many of them women, and reflecting their own individual experiences. For example, the Low Countries of Europe saw the emergence of the Beguines, lay women who organized themselves into sisterhoods, both large and small, and devoted themselves to lives of contemplation. Drawing upon the contemporary poetic style of courtly love they often described being ravished by God or by Jesus, whom they portrayed as a handsome young man.

However, it was the England of this period that produced some of the most influential of the medieval mystics. It is not hard to understand why. Europe, and England in particular, was in social and political turmoil in the fourteenth century. Internecine family squabbles in the court of Edward III led to political turmoil. Trouble with Scotland in the north and France to the east finally erupted into what was to become the Hundred Years War. Such a protracted war must inevitably exact a heavy financial toll on people and, as usual, the common folk bore the brunt of the burden of taxation. Meanwhile, much of the church was morally reprobate, with bishops living lives of ostentatious extravagance. Not surprisingly, resentment amongst the working class soon broke out into violence, and the Peasants Revolt erupted in 1381. One of the victims of the outbreaks was the Archbishop of Canterbury.

On the continent, the church was rent asunder in the Great Schism of 1377, as rival popes hurled abuse at each other and, eventually, took up arms to determine who was the sole and authorized Vicar of Christ. Reformers like John Wyclif and his followers, disparagingly labelled Lollards ('loafers'), opposed the corruption in the church, while at the same time working to get the Bible translated and available in the vernacular. They were condemned as heretics, and savagely persecuted and executed. All these traumatic events, though, paled in significance compared to what struck Europe in 1348. The Black Plague wiped out one-third of England, and up to a half of the population of Europe. There was a further outbreak in 1369. One can barely imagine the grief and terror which this scourge engendered, and it would have left deep emotional and psychological scars for decades.

Against such a tumultuous background England experienced a renewal of mysticism. The hermit Richard Rolle (ca.1290-1349) advocated the solitary life as the best means for experiencing God. His most famous work, *The Fire of Love*, described the stages he went through in experiencing Christ, each one marked by "an unusually pleasant heat", until he finally attained the heights of loving Christ. Rolle insisted that these sensations were real and physical. He wrote:

> It was real warmth, too, not imaginary, and it felt as if it were actually on fire. I was astonished at the way the heat surged up, and how this new sensation brought great and unexpected comfort. I had to keep feeling my breast to make sure there was no physical reason for it. But once I realized that it came entirely from within, that this love had no cause, material or sinful, but was the gift of my Maker, I was absolutely delighted, and wanted my love to be even greater.[4]

By contrast Walter Hilton (died 1396) rejected the idea that the life of solitary contemplation was the one best suited for the experience of God. A person could just as well attain complete love of God as a hermit or as an active member of a community. For him illumination came, not through bodily sensations or a heightened imagination, but through the Spirit enlightening human reason.

Nevertheless, while the path to illumination may have been different for Hilton, the ultimate goal was the same: the reforming of the lost image of God with a view to achieving perfect love. This century also saw, arguably, the greatest English mystic, Julian of Norwich, who wrote *Revelation of Love;* and the appearance of the perennial mystical classic, *The Cloud of Unknowing.*

Revelation of Love—Julian of Norwich

Of all the English mystics, the most quoted today is Lady Julian of Norwich (c. 1342–c.1413). Actually, we don't really know her name. Later in her life she became an anchoress, that is, she adopted the solitary life, living in a small room attached to St Julian's Church in Norwich—hence her name. Julian records that on May 8th, 1373, when she was "thirty and a half years old" she began to receive a series of sixteen showings, or revelations. Here, in her own words, is how it happened:

> God sent me a bodily sickness in which I lay for three days and three nights; and on the fourth night I took all my rites of holy Church and did not believe to live till day. After this I languished for two days and two nights ... After this my sight began to fail and it was all dark about me in the chamber as if it had been night, save in the image of the cross wherein I beheld a

common light, and I knew not how ... Now I felt truly I would die. Yet of a sudden, all my pain was taken away from me, and I was healthy again as before ... Now at once I saw red blood trickling down from under the garland. Hot and freely it fell, copious and real it was, as if it had been just pressed down upon his blessed head.[5]

It is obvious that Julian had long been a devout and earnest Christian. She writes that, before receiving these revelations, she had been gripped by three desires. Firstly, she had longed to understand more of the sufferings of Christ so that she might know more of the pain that he endured, and his compassion for those whom he loves. Secondly, when thirty years of age, she had desired to have a bodily sickness that would be to the point of death, so that she might be thoroughly purged and then be with her God. Finally, she desired of God three wounds: "the wound of true contrition, the wound of kind compassion, and the wound of wilful longing for God". *Revelation of Love* describes how God graciously granted Julian each of her desires.

How did Julian receive these showings? She mentions three modes of revelation. We have already seen that she described how graphic and vivid her visions of the death of Christ were. She saw so much blood that, had it been real, the floor would have been awash with it. She saw Christ's face covered with dried blood. She felt the force of a cold, dry wind that swept over his dying body. As well as these bodily visions, Julian also records that there were "words given directly to my understanding". For example, having witnessed Christ's sufferings, Julian records that Jesus spoke to her and said, "This is my joy, my bliss, my endless liking that I was ever able to suffer for you. Truly, if I could have suffered more, I would have suffered more".[6] Finally, she received revelation through "spiritual enlightenment". In other words, in the years that followed the reception of these showings she reflected on what had been revealed to her, and came to a fuller understanding of its meaning. So, for example, she writes, "I saw and understood by the Lord's meaning that in this life we may not keep ourselves from sin as holy and fully clean as we will in heaven".[7]

It is clear that there are two sources of authority for Julian: the teachings of the church and the revelations she has received. What happens should these two authorities conflict? As we will see, a large part of the book is an exploration of this very issue. At the same time, it is striking how few references there are to the word of God in *Revelation of Love*. There are biblical allusions, and the occasional quote (such as Jesus' words from the cross, "I thirst"), and a statement that God's word teaches the damnation of the fallen angels, the heathen, and ungodly Christians.[8] Nevertheless, the two authorities that Julian finds herself bound to submit to are the received teachings of the Church and the personal revelations she has been given.

In order to appreciate the attraction that this book holds for many today we need to explore something of Julian's spirituality. The first thing that strikes the reader is Julian's intense longing for intimacy with God:

> For until I am fully one with him, I can never have full rest nor true bliss; that is to say, until I am so at one with him that no thing created comes between us, my God and me.[9]

God for her is pure, unbounding love. No one can fathom how sweetly and tenderly God loves them. Julian speaks of her experience of God's love in the most tender and personal way. When the Lord expresses to her his love, it is as if he is saying to her, "My darling, behold and see your God, who is your Maker and your endless joy; see what liking and bliss I have in your salvation, and for my love enjoy now with me".[10] Indeed, so deep and rich is God's love for his "Lovers", that it seems that our longing for intimacy with him is matched by his desire for us: "our Lover desires the soul to stay close to him with all its strength, clinging ever more tightly to his goodness".[11]

Given that this revelation of God's love is so intense and so all-embracing, it is not surprising that Julian can find no place in the heart of such a God for anger or accusation. Julian grapples with the age-old problem of pain. God has revealed to her that "all things will be well", yet the reality is that great harm comes to his creatures. Why did God allow sin into the world in the first place? In particular, Julian's revelations have convinced her that there is no wrath in God: "It is utterly impossible that God should be wrath. For wrath and friendship are two opposites". This, however, places her on the horns of a dilemma. Her visions of God have shown her a God who is empty of wrath and, therefore, a God who assigns no blame to his people ("between God and our soul there is neither wrath nor need for forgiveness in his sight"). Yet, at the same time, her church clearly teaches that she must confess herself a sinner, deserving of blame and wrath. A significant part of *Revelation of Love* records Julian's attempt to resolve this paradox.

The answer came to Julian in a parable the Lord gave her. A lord once sent a loving, zealous servant on an errand. In his haste to do his master's will, the servant fell into a boggy dell and was badly hurt. There he lay in darkness, moaning and groaning, and unable to extract himself. This fall led to great pain, and to his senses being stunned. As a consequence, he forgot his Lord's love for him. Julian then poses the question, is the servant in any way at fault because of this fall? Julian could see no fault, "for it was only his good will and great willingness that had caused his falling".[12]

Julian's parable had a twofold application. Firstly, the servant is Adam and, therefore, all of us, since we are all Adam. By Adam's fall we have been enfeebled, stunned in our understanding, and kept from beholding God. This is man's shame and sin. Broken and fractured, a person then acts in ways contrary to the will of God. The servant's good will remains intact ("For in every soul that shall be saved is a godly will that never assents to sin"), but his understanding is impaired and he feels hurt and isolated. However, since all this is the result of a fall, God cannot be angry with us and does not apportion any blame to us. At the same time, this servant is also Jesus, who fell into Mary's womb, which is the valley of this wretched world, and he did so that he might lift us out of it.

How, then, does this resolve Julian's dilemma? The church, rightly, attaches blame to sin, since sin is the consequence of the fracture that has resulted from the fall. God, though, looks at the good heart of the servant who, through no fault of his own, but simply desiring to do the Lord's will, fell and became blind and broken.

Finally, some comments need to be made about one of the most unusual, and original, perspectives that Julian brings to her understanding of God, and that is on the Motherhood of

Jesus! While holding to a traditional Trinitarian understanding of God as Father, Son, and Spirit she also sees the Trinity in terms of God the Father, Jesus our Mother, and the Spirit as our Lord. She writes,

> In the first I saw that the high might of the Trinity is our Father; and the deep wisdom of the Trinity is our Mother; and the great love of the Trinity is our Lord.[13]

Jesus is our Mother, and "our true Mother" because, as a mother, he both brings us to birth, and feeds and protects us. She writes,

> We well know that all our mothers bear us to pain and to dying. Yet what does he do? Our own true Mother Jesus, he who is all love, bears us to joy and endless living. Thus he sustains us within himself in love and labour until the full time when he gladly suffered the sharpest throes and most grievous pains that ever where or ever shall be, and died at last ... The mother may suckle her children with her own milk, but our precious Mother Jesus, he may feed us with himself. And he does this most courteously, with much tenderness, with the Blessed Sacrament that is our precious food of true life.[14]

It is not difficult to see the appeal that Julian's spirituality would have to people today. While her reclusive lifestyle would strike many as extreme, even unhealthy and bizarre, both her experience of God and her theological understanding of what God is like, which is directly informed by her experience, would be very attractive. God for her is not some remote theological principle, but a personal encounter. To people hungry for love, Julian's God offers a love that is totally accepting and without condemnation. In a society of fragmented family relationships, where parental abuse of children seems to be of almost epidemic proportions, and where many children spend much of their early years in child care centres, or are shuttled between parents who no longer live together, Julian from her experience brings a new type of understanding of the biblical truth that God is perfect Father and Mother, who goes to any lengths of self-sacrifice to demonstrate unlimited, unconditional love.

Julian's God is not a God to fear, but a God to whom you surrender, as to a lover, so that his passionate absorption with you might embrace and engulf you. While Julian is still bound to the teachings of her church, with serious repercussions should she dispute them, in the end it is her own experience of God that becomes the interpretive grid for her received beliefs about God. The church may have taught her to believe in hell, sin, and judgement, but Julian is able to reinterpret these terms so that they are consistent with the one fact about God which, for her, is irrefutable: in him is no wrath.

The Cloud of Unknowing

Another great mystical classic from the same period is the anonymous *The Cloud of Unknowing*. Virtually nothing is known about the author of this influential work. It is worth comparing this book with *Revelation of Love* because, while they come from the same time and place, they present very different styles of mysticism. Indeed, in parts *The Cloud* is scathingly critical of the sort of visionary experiences that are so integral to the spirituality of people like Julian.

The Cloud belongs firmly in what is called the 'apophatic' tradition of mysticism which argues paradoxically that the less you know about God, the more you know, and the more your knowledge of God is wrapped in darkness, the closer you are to the light. In chapter 3 of his book, the author introduces his theme, the great work which God wants people to do:

> And see to it that you have no wish to think on anything but God himself, so that nothing engages your mind or your will except him. And do your best to forget all the created things that God ever made and all their works ... This is the work of the soul which most pleases God ... Do not let up then, but labour at it until you feel longing. For the first time you do you find only darkness and, as it were, a cloud of unknowing.[15]

According to the author, all thoughts about God, even about his works and attributes, while good in themselves, are ultimately distractions that will not lead to God. God is only experienced and apprehended by love. He advised that the contemplative soul "must smite upon that thick cloud of unknowing with a sharp dart of longing love, and not leave it whatever happens" (p. 10). Since God is incomprehensible to thoughts, one should approach him with wordlessness. Indeed, simple cries of one syllable are sufficient. Using the analogy of the man in danger who simply cries out "Help!" and "Fire!" and for whom more words would be both unnecessary and counter-productive, so the simple cry, "God" or "Love" is sufficient for the supplicant.

If the author is dismissive of thinking or knowing as a means of comprehending God, he is acerbic in his comments about those who speak of visionary experiences. In a non-too-subtle reference to Robert Rolle, he warns against those who have

> their breasts inflamed with an unnatural heat caused
> by misuse of their bodies in this pretended work; or
> else they conceive a false heat engendered by the devil,
> their spiritual enemy, caused by their pride, sensuality
> and speculative mind. And yet perhaps they think that
> it is the fire of love.[16]

With a mockery that would have done Martin Luther proud he describes such charlatans as having "a fixed stare as if they were sheep affected by a brain disease", or sitting "with their mouths gaping as if they were catching flies". Such pretences of holiness, for this author, are nothing more than fiendish mental delusions.

The author's caustic attacks on claimants to such divine encounters must not be taken to suggest that his spirituality is less than experiential. The author recognizes that should a soul labour long and hard to pierce the cloud of unknowing, then by grace God may reward him with a taste of heaven.

> (God) will perhaps, at some time, send out a beam of
> spiritual light that pierces the cloud of unknowing that
> is between you and him, and show you some of his
> secrets which no man can nor may put into words.
> Then you will feel your affection ablaze with the fire of
> his love, far more than I can tell you.[17]

It is clear that the author of this work sees the contemplative life as the highest form of devotion and, in fact, the only life that makes possible the sort of spiritual work which this book commends. Just as the path of theological reflection is a spiritual dead end, so the active life, a life comprising deeds of service, is inadequate as a means of reaching spiritual perfection. At length the author allegorically points to Jesus' friends, Martha and Mary, as exemplifying the two kinds of spiritual life. The former works for her Lord, complaining about her sister's inactivity. While the portion she has chosen is a good one, it is not the best, and it does not draw her close to the heart of her Lord. Mary by contrast is the contemplative, who simply sits and listens, focussing on her Lord with pure love. She has chosen the best portion "because the perfect impulse of love that begins here is equal in all respects to that which will last forever in the bliss of heaven".[18]

While very different from Julian of Norwich, the heart of both spiritualities is one and the same: an encounter with divine love. *The Cloud* is liberally sprinkled with references to scripture, and the author clearly sees his book as consistent with the teachings of the church. Nevertheless, for him, as for Julian, the pathway to the true knowledge of God is not via theological propositions, but by being open to encounters of divine love. It is an encounter where words are virtually superfluous, if not actually being obstacles to perfect union with God.

Many have noted the similarities between the spirituality of this anonymous author and Zen Buddhism. Zen masters counsel devotees to abandon their bodies and souls into the abundance of light, and drive from their minds any and all distractions which keep them from the light. Once words are abandoned, and divine shafts of light are the medium of revelation and experience, then theological differences become superfluous. It is no wonder that some have seen writings like *The Cloud* as important points of contact between Christianity and other religions.

Further, people today are feeling increasingly stressed by the sheer volume of activities that fill their days, and place demands on their time. Christians find this same hectic pace reflected in their church life. With an endless round of meetings and gatherings, and always more jobs to be done than people willing to do them, committed Christians complain of spiritual burnout. They feel like modern-day Marthas, enviously eyeing their serene sisters and wishing that they, too, had chosen that portion which seems to have brought them so much closer to the Lord they both love. To such soul seekers, a spirituality that sees passivity and quietness as a more excellent way, over and against the way of religious activity, will seem compelling and appealing.

Mysticism in the late middle ages

Mysticism flourished all over Europe, but sixteenth-century Spain was another of the high water marks of the tradition, boasting such notable mystical thinkers as Ignatius Loyola, St John of the Cross and, especially, Teresa of Avila. Few mystics have gained more popular renown in recent years than the Spanish Carmelite nun, Teresa of Avila (1515–1582). It is not surprising that many have been attracted to the warm, conversational style of this very likeable contemplative. There is no hint of pretence in Teresa's writings. She regularly apologizes for digressing from her theme, or repeating herself, or forgetting where precisely in the Bible something was written ("now was it Jesus or Paul?"). With characteristic self-effacement she even gives the reader forewarning when she's about to write something worthwhile: "This chapter has some good points", she wryly comments in some introductory remarks. Despite a difficult life (she eventually died just worn out), it seems that she never lost her sense of humour, or her very deep and genuine love for her Lord and for others.

The Interior Castle—Teresa of Avila

One her best known books, *The Interior Castle*, is a description of the seven stages of prayer, called the Seven Dwelling Places, which lead to intimate union with God. She selects a castle as a metaphor for the human soul:

> It is that we consider our soul to be a castle made entirely out of a diamond or of very clear crystal, in which there are many rooms, just as in heaven there are many dwelling places ... what do you think that abode will be like where a King so powerful, so wise, so pure, so full of all good things takes His delight? I don't find anything comparable to the magnificent beauty of a soul and its marvellous capacity.[19]

Prayer is the gate of entry into the castle and, as we have seen in other writings, progress towards deeper union with God only comes through much effort: "True union can very well be reached, with God's help, if we make the effort to obtain it by keeping our wills fixed only on that which is God's will".[20] The further one proceeds on this journey inwards, the more one must dispense with the intellect. Teresa advises,

> In order to profit by this path and ascend to the dwelling places we desire, the important thing is not to think much but to love much.[21]

The Lord also has other ways of awakening the soul:

unexpectedly when it is praying vocally and not thinking of anything interior, it seems a delightful enkindling will come upon it as though a fragrance were suddenly to become so powerful as to spread through all the senses.[22]

During her life Teresa frequently enjoyed mystical experiences such as visions and ecstatic raptures. While being aware that these can sometimes be delusory, she felt sure one could discern the genuine from the spurious. The closer one draws to union with God, the more such raptures might occur. Once one reaches the Fourth Dwelling Place, then "supernatural experiences begin here. Since these dwelling places now are closer to where the King is, their beauty is great. There are things to see and understand that the intellect is incapable of devising a way to explain".[23] By the Sixth Dwelling Place the references to different kinds of visions become more frequent:

When the soul is in suspension, the Lord likes to show it some secrets, things about heaven, and imaginative visions. It is able to tell of them afterward, for these remain so impressed on the memory that they are never forgotten.[24]

What, then, is the nature of this final union with God, should one be blessed enough to attain it? It is a state of being in habitual remembrance of God, feeling like one is always walking with him. It is nothing less than a touch of heaven:

What God communicates here to the soul in an instant is a secret so great and a favour so sublime— and the delight the soul experiences so extreme—that I don't know what to compare it to. I can only say that the Lord wishes to reveal for that moment ... the glory of heaven."[25]

The deepest longing of the human heart is to live by sight and not by faith. To see, if not with the exterior eye, then at least with internal vision, the glory of the life to come. Teresa, consistent with other mystics, insists that this experience can be enjoyed here and now. It will take effort, and perhaps a lifetime of effort. It will be very difficult to find apart from a life of contemplation. And it will be only for a select few. Indeed, she (mis)quotes Matthew 22:14, "Many are called but few are chosen". It is quite clear that by these words Jesus was referring to all his disciples, but in the mystical tradition the elect are those few among the followers of Jesus who attain the heights of ecstatic union with God.

The Practice of the Presence of God—Brother Lawrence

Any treatment of the classics of the mystical tradition would be incomplete without a reference to *The Practice of the Presence of God*. If the writings of the likes of Lady Julian and Teresa of Avila are unfamiliar to many evangelical Christians, the same cannot be said of Brother Lawrence's popular classic. While it is referred to more often as a devotional classic than a mystical one (presumably because the former term is a more acceptable one to an evangelical audience than the latter), we will see that it really is hewn from the same rock as the other mystical writings we have surveyed.

Brother Lawrence (1611-1691) was an ex-soldier who after his conversion joined the Carmelite order and worked in the kitchen of a monastery near Paris. *The Practice of the Presence of God* is a collection of conversations, letters, and spiritual principles written towards the end of his life. For Lawrence, the sum total of the spiritual life is the presence of God. "If I were a preacher", he writes, "I would preach nothing else but the practice of the presence of God".[26] What is the presence of God? Lawrence writes:

> I try to keep myself always in God's holy presence by simple attentiveness and a loving gaze upon him. This I may call the actual presence of God, or to speak more accurately, an habitual, silent and hidden communion of the soul with Him.[27]

It is having one's thoughts being lifted above earthly things and being in a state of constant communion with Him. The goal is a state in which the believer's thoughts are always and only of God, being able to banish every other thought or temptation as soon as it approaches. Over time, with practice, some will reach the position where this sense of his presence is continual and uninterrupted. Is it something tangible? Lawrence doesn't speak of dreams or visions or hearing the voice of God, but his sense of God's presence is profoundly experiential. In his section "Of the Union of the Soul with God", he writes:

> Yet our feelings can deceive us as to this union, for it is not merely an emotion ... It is rather *an undefinable something of the soul* ... it lifts the soul up to God, impelling her to love him, to worship Him, even to embrace Him with caresses *which cannot be expressed and which only experience can make us understand.*[28]

Indeed, the soul may reach such a state of perfection that it can almost say, "I no longer believe, for I can see and experience".[29]

How does one capture this sense of God's presence? Like other mystics, there is an emphasis on human effort, in particular the driving out of one's mind any contrary thoughts and focussing solely on God's love. Without going to the lengths of the author of *The Cloud*, who counsels forgetting everything, Lawrence still believed that "our thoughts spoil everything, all the trouble begins with them. We must be careful to reject them immediately".[30] Similarly, penitential practices and mortifications were also of limited spiritual value. Union with God is obtained through love: "the shortest way to come to God was by a continual exercise of love, doing all things for his sake".[31]

While prayer is central to this life of union with God, again words can be more of a hindrance than a help. Lawrence counsels the seeker to use short ejaculations, such as "My God, I am wholly yours ... or any other such words as love may suggest at the moment".[32] Long speeches, by contrast, often induce distractions. So, one must control one's thoughts in prayer, riveting the attention to the presence of God.

One of the great appeals of Brother Lawrence's classic is that it advocates a spirituality for the ordinary and everyday. One can realize this divine presence anywhere and everywhere. One does not need to go to church; "we make a chapel of our hearts". One does not need to be involved in religious practice. Lawrence experienced this presence daily in his work in the kitchen. This is because the home of spirituality is the human heart. Lawrence counsels,

Since you know that God is with you in all your actions, that He is at the very depth and centre of your soul, why not then pause an instant in your external occupations, and even in your prayers, to worship Him inwardly, to praise Him, to petition Him.[33]

Once again, as with other mystical classics, the level of intimacy of union with God being presented here is only for the chosen few. Lawrence concludes his "Spiritual Principles" by acknowledging that "only a few persons attain this state; it is a grace which God bestows on certain chosen souls". As for the rest, well, they can get close "with the assistance of ordinary grace and by the practice of the presence of God".[34]

One of the first things that strikes you about Brother Lawrence's practice of God's presence is what is absent. His spirituality is thoroughly God-focussed, with little reference to the Lord Jesus Christ. Indeed, the virtual absence of Jesus may explain some of the more disturbing aspects of his theology. Lawrence openly admits his uncertainties about his own salvation. Reflecting traditional medieval Catholic theology, he anticipates the purging of his sins after death and the hope of final salvation. "Whether I am lost or saved", he writes, "I want simply to go on living entirely for God".[35] Any assurance he has of God's final acceptance is rooted in his experience of God's love.

More worrying is that those spiritual blessings which are the fruit of the finished work of Christ, Lawrence attributes to his own spiritual efforts. For example, he writes that "by such unceasing turning to God we shall crush the head of Satan and strike his weapons from His hands".[36] Whereas scripture affirms that Christ's once-for-all victory on the cross crushed

Satan's head, won our salvation, and ushered us into the presence of God, for Brother Lawrence these blessings seem to be even more the consequence of the union with Christ which he enjoys because of his own spiritual discipline.

This comes to the heart of what is so disturbing about this Christian classic, and its enthusiastic embracing by many Christians. The very premise of the book is that the presence of God is something that eludes Christians, or is only experienced fleetingly by the majority of them. It is only by persistent hard work, which is then met by God's grace, that this level of union can be experienced. This cuts right across the glorious, liberating news of the gospel. One of the great blessings of the gospel is that, because of Christ's death, we are in Christ, living daily in his presence. We cannot be more in his presence on one day than another, and one believer cannot more be in his Lord's presence than another.

THIS HAS BEEN just a thumbnail sketch of a few of the mystical classics. I wanted you to hear them for themselves, in their own words, with a minimum of critical comment or appraisal. But we need to think more critically about what they are saying and the kind of spirituality that they are advocating. We need to examine further their modern-day appeal, particularly to those who are evangelical Christians, because there is no denying the fact that the mystics are touching a receptive chord in many human hearts.

ENDNOTES

1   Tacey, *The Spirituality Revolution*, p. 193.
2   Evelyn Underhill, *Mystics of the Church*, James Clarke, Cambridge, 1925, p. 27.
3   For a recent, excellent historical survey of mysticism see Steven Fanning's *Mystics of the Christian Tradition*, Routledge, London, 2001. I am indebted to Fanning for much of my material in this section.
4   See the account in Fanning, *Mystics*, pp. 119-121.
5   *A Revelation of Love*, pp. 5-7. Shortly after receiving these revelations, Julian wrote them down in what has become known as the Short Text of *A Revelation of Love*. It seems that some time after this she became an anchoress and for the next twenty years reflected further on the meaning of these showings, and then wrote a fuller account of what she had received. This is referred to as the Long Text. We are using the Long Text translated by John Skinner (Image Books, New York, 1996).
6   *Revelation of Love*, p. 22.
7   *Revelation of Love*, p. 115.
8   *Revelation of Love*, p. 63.
9   *Revelation of Love*, p. 5.
10 *Revelation of Love*, p. 50.
11 *Revelation of Love*, p. 13.
12 *Revelation of Love*, p. 101.
13 *Revelation of Love*, p. 129.
14 *Revelation of Love*, p. 134.
15 Robert Way, *The Cloud of Unknowing*, Source Books, Trabuco Canyon/ Anthony Clarke, Wheathamstead, 1986, pp. 11-12.
16 *The Cloud of Unknowing*, p. 70.
17 *The Cloud of Unknowing*, p. 49.
18 *The Cloud of Unknowing*, p. 41.
19 Teresa of Avila, *The Interior Castle*, Trans. Kieran Kavanaugh & Otilio Rodriguez, Library of Western Spirituality, Paulist Press, New York, 1979, p. 35.
20 *The Interior Castle*, p. 98.
21 *The Interior Castle*, p. 70.
22 *The Interior Castle*, p. 118.
23 *The Interior Castle*, p. 67.
24 *The Interior Castle*, p. 128.

25 *The Interior Castle*, p. 178.

26 We are following the translation by Donald Attwater, *The Practice of the Presence of God*, Templegate, Springfield, 1974, p. 61.

27 *The Practice of the Presence of God*, pp. 73-74.

28 *The Practice of the Presence of God*, p. 117 (italics mine).

29 *The Practice of the Presence of God*, p. 125.

30 *The Practice of the Presence of God*, p. 38.

31 *The Practice of the Presence of God*, pp. 39-40.

32 *The Practice of the Presence of God*, p. 123.

33 *The Practice of the Presence of God*, p. 112.

34 *The Practice of the Presence of God*, p. 126.

35 *The Practice of the Presence of God*, p. 35.

36 *The Practice of the Presence of God*, p. 111.

Chapter 7

The Lure of Mysticism

PEOPLE LONG TO be connected to God and, through him, to others, and even to the world around them, and mysticism holds out the promise here and now of such a deep, intimate relationship. Mystics, then and now, don't just talk about God, they talk to God—and often hear him talking to them. And the God the mystics encounter is the God of unconditional, total, self-giving love. Further, the love of this God is less an objective reality, which finds its expression in historical events like the life, death, and resurrection of Jesus Christ, but a subjective awareness of divine affection and acceptance.

Mysticism, by its very nature, is inclusive. Each year up to 100,000 Christians from Catholic, charismatic, and evangelical backgrounds put aside their theological differences and visit retreat centres like Taize (in the Burgundy district of France) to pursue the ancient traditions of prayer. Day after day, worshippers sit or kneel in a darkened room, facing ceiling to floor banners, with hundreds of flickering candles and icons, while they participate in chanting, hour-long Bible studies, and prolonged times of silence.[1]

Mystical experiences may not just connect Christians from different ecclesiastical traditions, but even people of different religious backgrounds. People may feel that they have had an encounter with the divine in their inner being which connects them with God. There may be much about their lives which is confusing, and they may have intellectual doubts about some of the teachings of their faith, but of this one thing they can be sure: they have met, known, and experienced God. They now meet other people, perhaps of other Christian traditions, or even other religions, who testify to similar experiences in their lives. Immediately, there is a point of contact and connection. If propositional truth lies at the heart of your faith then inevitably there will be conflict with people who reject your propositions about God. It is hard to have genuine unity and connectedness when there is a wall of rival truth claims that divide you. However, if a subjective encounter with God lies at the heart of your spiritual life then you can connect more easily with people with whom you might differ theologically. Further, if wordlessness marks the character of your prayerful communion with God, then doctrine becomes less important. For mystics, spirituality is fundamentally about a subjective sense of union with God, not cognitive adherence to objective truths. Knowing God is something you feel and experience, not something you've studied and learnt. This subjective union with God breeds a sense of kinship with others who feel the same sense of connectedness.

Related to this, mysticism brings with it a democratization of the Spirit. In evangelicalism, the leader or mentor is often the theologically trained 'expert' on the Bible. He, and normally the leader is a male, is recognized to have leadership gifts and is usually required to be intellectually a cut or two above the average. Very few non-graduates exercise authority in a congregation. However, mystical experiences, while often granted to a select few, are given to people without regard for age, gender or academic ability. And the reception of such an experience catapults the mystic into a position of power, influence, and respect. They have met God and, perhaps, heard the voice of God and now can speak of this God with authority.

Celebrating the disciplines: evangelicals and mysticism

For centuries mysticism has held a strong appeal for Christians, but it has generally found a home amongst people of the Catholic and Orthodox traditions. While some evangelicals have acquainted themselves with mystical writings, the fact that the mystics have been 'tarred with the Roman brush' have made most people wary of venturing too far into these unfamiliar waters.

However, recently this has begun to change. Increasingly, evangelical writers are calling upon people to put aside their uninformed prejudices and give the mystics a fresh look. These writers are often speaking out of an experience of spiritual dryness due, they say, to the spiritually and emotionally barren kind of evangelical piety that they have been brought up with. These Christians testify to the fact that evangelicalism, with its emphasis on the intellect and the study of the Bible, leaves them parched and dry. They need renewal and refreshment.

The mystical tradition and the charismatic tradition are, spiritually, close cousins.[2] While the particular expression of one's experience may differ, the fact remains that people now claim to have had a life-changing subjective encounter with God, unlike anything they had known before. This immediately creates a connection with like-experienced (as opposed to like-minded) other people. Increasingly, evangelical writers are suggesting that the much-neglected mystical tradition of the church can be mined, and nuggets of spiritual truth extracted which will transform one's spiritual life.

For Christians who are tired of occasional, perfunctory prayer times there is the promise of a way of prayer that is powerfully engaging. For evangelicals who are tired of having to drag themselves to predictable, uninspiring church services, here is a spirituality that will make you long each week, or even each day, for an encounter with God.

Tommy Tenney in his book *The God Catchers: Experiencing the Manifest Presence of God*, writes that, "Ever since He touched me, I go to every church meeting, worship service, and prayer gathering, saying 'I wonder if this will be the night He will show up again?'"[3] Mind you, Tenney admits that since he was caught by God and "something that was always there in another dimension" suddenly entered his life, then from that point on church was ruined for him. The sermons and the songs now made him sick, because he had experienced the excitement of God's presence.

Bruce Demarest is an American evangelical writer and seminary professor. He is theologically orthodox and his conservative credentials are impeccable, having trained and taught in some of North America's leading seminaries. He has been a missionary and student worker. His writings are published by respected evangelical publishing houses. And for most of his Christian life he confesses that his life lacked power and a sense of the presence of God. In his own words, this is Demarest's *before* experience:

> From outward experiences my life and ministry were above reproach and 'successful'. A flow of notes from seminary students and graduates expressed appreciation for my teaching and defense of the faith. In retrospect, I admit I was a typical product of evangelical academic culture ... I tended to view the Christian faith largely in terms of rational propositions, so I loaded (and probably overloaded) my mind with intellectual analysis. True, I could wax eloquent about the mysteries of the Trinity, or theories about the Atonement, but I didn't relate that well to God on an

everyday, affective level. I substituted knowledge of the Bible for knowing how to interact with God himself ... My evangelical culture and training led me to this belief: Personal experience is an untrustworthy pillar for Christian faith and life. Therefore you should relegate life and matters of the heart to an inferior place.[4]

Then an Episcopalian renewal team visited Bruce's church, taking sessions which showed people how actually to experience God in their lives, and have their souls renewed. These men introduced people to the mystics, and now for the first time in a long while Demarest "experienced the sense of actual growth in the inner man". Then he attended a six-week residential programme at a Benedictine Abbey. Although the folk who attended were from different traditions, they were united in their search for a deeper connectedness with Christ. This is Demarest's *after* experience:

> Our days at Pesos were centred around practising God's presence, stimulated by three worship services per day; the morning Eucharist, afternoon prayers, and evening vespers. Again, as each day's lectures plumbed the heart of the spiritual life, I found myself stimulated and moved ... I became as aware of God as I'd ever been, during quiet walks under pristine skies and rugged mountains. At the end of the six weeks, virtually everyone—Catholic, Anglican, charismatic, and evangelical—testified to the many true ways the experience had transformed his or her spirit and life (p. 31).

Demarest returned to his seminary transformed, and his classes "came to life". Before, he was part of the great evangelical majority who knew about God, and believed that the path to a deeper knowledge of God was the amassing of more information about him. Now, he is part of the smaller group which differs from the ordinary orthodox Christian only because he "experiences his faith down in the depths of his sentient being while the other does not".[5] The avenue to such renewal for him, and the others, was the medieval spiritual disciplines of the mystics. He realized that, for all the good they had done, the Reformers, in their rejection of mystics, had thrown out the spiritual baby with the theological bathwater. Further, he discovered there was a way of engaging with God which was intuitive rather than intellectual, and which opened the heart as well as the head to truth.

Firstly, Demarest advocates the *discipline of meditation*. Meditation "refocuses us from ourselves and from the world so that we may reflect on God's word". Meditation is not Bible study. It is not reading the Bible in order to prepare a talk, or come to grips with some theological issue. There is a place for such approaches to the scripture, but meditation is a thoughtful reflecting upon scripture and allowing that scripture so to penetrate your inner being that you are transformed by it. This is what we saw Kathleen Norris describing earlier in her popular book *The Cloister Walk*. She calls this kind of meditation 'spiritual reading'. It is a slow, meditative reading which allows the words, which resonate with the full range of human experience, to "flow freely, to wash over you".[6] While, for Demarest, scripture is the primary focus of one's meditation, one may also, with spiritual benefit, meditate on other Christian writings, hymns, religious art and icons.

Hand in hand with meditation, is entrance into the *discipline of silence*. Elijah, it is said, could only hear the voice of

God, and receive comfort and direction for his life, when all was quiet and he listened to the still, small voice. This is seen as paradigmatic for the believer today. In our frenetic lives, where our mind and soul are bombarded by stimulants and demands, it is impossible to discern the voice of God amidst all the din. We need to get away. We, too, must retreat to a lonely place, and in the stillness, hear the silence of God's voice. In the famous words of the psalmist, "Be still and know that I am God" (Ps 46:10).

Often confused by many people with meditation is the *discipline of contemplation*, but it differs in that the focus of attention is not necessarily a book or a picture about God, but God himself. It is "fixing the eyes of the inner man on God Himself". This is the practice of God's presence. It often expresses itself in contemplative prayer. What marks this prayer as special is its brevity. Demarest endorses the practice of the mystics in prayer, who selected just one phrase and repeated it over and over again. Such a practice, which he distinguishes from the pagan mantra, helps draw important aspects of God's being deep into the heart, so creating an inner stillness and enabling the supplicant to hear the voice of God. Related to this, Demarest encourages Christians to involve all of their bodies in the act of worship—not just the mind. The smell of flowers and incense, the sound of a bell, a picture of Christ, the taste of bread and wine, all help us to relate to God in a more meaningful way.

Much more could be said about the spiritual disciplines. One could mention the practice of fasting, journalling, spiritual mentoring, and confession. Demarest gently rebukes those evangelicals, from the Reformers on, who have dismissed the mystics because of their occasional, and undeniable, theological blind spots. He encourages us to walk with others on a journey inward, focussing on our soul, which is the seat of our spiritual life. This inward journey is made possible by turning back, mining the mystics for the spiritual gems which God revealed to them for our edification.

Reflections on the mystics

One of the great services that the current resurgence in mysticism has done for us is that it has challenged us to stop and think again about our rollercoaster Christian lives and ask ourselves, is this how it is meant to be? Is workaholism a fruit of the Spirit? Is busyness the mark of true dedication to Christ? Is filling our minds with more Christian words necessarily the path to understanding and maturity?

However, we must pause to think critically and biblically about the sort of advice that is being given to us today regarding the mystics. For people who feel spiritually dry, the prospect of a spiritual oasis is an appealing one. But are the waters of its pool fresh or polluted? Do they really satisfy the soul? And is there a hidden price tag? Our survey of some of the mystical classics ought to have demonstrated that there are very serious theological concerns in the kind of spirituality that is being offered.

Of course, you might well respond that this is a typical and predictable response. Just when people have experienced something which they have found real and meaningful, nitpickers want to cut theological holes in it. When people want a dynamic encounter with the living God, spiritual wet rags keep wanting to douse the flames of zeal with cries of 'theological foul'! In fact, someone might even go as far as to say that that's just the problem with some Christians today: too much theology!

It goes without saying that the church has often been weakened and disempowered by a dead orthodoxy or dry formalism. There have always been immature Christians who have inhibited their own spiritual growth, and the maturing of others, through endless debates over secondary issues. But we must never despise the exercise of proper theological investigation because some have abused this activity. Theology is just a succinct term for the search for truth about God. If we are raising theological questions we are raising questions of truth, and therefore of virtue. If the Lord has told us about himself and how he wants us to relate to him, then we will want to listen to him, and listen to him carefully. We will want to respond to him in the way that best pleases him, and therefore in the way which will both change and transform us, and bring us the most God-honouring joy. The 19th-century missionary Henry Martyn wrote that "I could not endure existence if Jesus was not glorified". Yet here are mystical classics where the Lord of glory is barely mentioned, and the benefits of his atoning death are misunderstood or marginalized. Does it really please and honour the Father when the Son is marginalized in books that purport to be pathways to Christian maturity and a genuine encounter with God?

While mystical exercises like contemplation, meditation, and silence may, superficially, seem to be consistent with traditional evangelical practices, we must not necessarily assume that because two traditions use the same words, then these words are referring to the same activity. The deconstructionists of postmodernism have rightly alerted us to how slippery words can be. Let's explore some of these terms.

Christian meditation

Meditation is a biblical practice which, today, few Christians have time for. The psalmist writes, "I will ponder all your work, and meditate on your mighty deeds" (77:12), and "I will meditate on your precepts and fix my eyes on your ways" (119:15). As Psalm 119 implies, the focus of Christian meditation is the word of God, the Lord's self-revelation of his character and his deeds. However, the heavens do declare God's glory and day after day they pour forth speech. To the mind enlightened by the Spirit and informed by the word of God, meditation on the splendour of God's creative genius can be profoundly enriching. Scientists continue to discover more about the wonders of creation, such as the magnitude of the universe, and the intricacies of DNA, and the fantastic variety of the animal kingdom. These expressions of the wisdom, power, and majesty of God ought to be reflected and meditated upon, to the glory of God.

There is an important place in the Christian life for deep reflection on God's words, pondering their implications for our knowledge of God, and how this affects our lives. However, in such meditation one doesn't dispense with the principles of biblical interpretation simply because this is a spiritual discipline. It is not as if, when preparing a Bible study, we employ all the principles of hermeneutics, such as sensitivity to the wider context, and paying attention to matters of genre and style and so on, but when we meditate on the word we put such principles aside, extract a verse out of its context and then let it sink deep into our soul. This is both an irresponsible way to treat holy scripture, as well as a recipe for error.

The sound of silence

What of the place of silence and solitude in the Christian life?
We have seen that for the ancient and medieval mystics, solitude was virtually essential so that the believer could hear the
unspoken voice of God and enter deeply into his presence.
Certainly, at crucial times in his life and ministry, the Lord
Jesus withdrew from the crowds which were constantly
pressing upon him, to a quiet and lonely place so that he
could commune with his Father. The quiet time has been a
cherished part of evangelical piety for generations. Christians
are encouraged to find, each day, a place where they can be
alone and remain uninterrupted, and there give themselves
to prayer and Bible reading. However, is this what the mystics
mean by silent solitude?

Reference is often made to Elijah's encounter with God on
Mt Horeb. Here's how the ancient narrator records the event,

> [At Mt Horeb] he came to a cave and lodged in it ...
> [God] said, "Go out and stand on the mount before the
> LORD." And behold, the LORD passed by, and a great
> and strong wind tore the mountains and broke in
> pieces the rocks before the LORD, but the Lord was not
> in the wind. And after the wind an earthquake, but the
> LORD was not in the earthquake. And after the earth-
> quake a fire, but the LORD was not in the fire. And
> after the fire the sound of a low whisper. And when
> Elijah heard it, he wrapped his face in his cloak
> and went out and stood at the entrance of the cave.
> And behold, there came a voice to him and said,
> "What are you doing here, Elijah? ... Go, return on
> your way ..." (1 Kings 19:9-15).

Richard Foster argues that we see here that "Elijah spent many a day and night in the wilderness learning to discern the 'still small voice of God'". But look at the passage again. Carefully. Is that what is happening here? Despite his triumph on Mt Carmel, Elijah flees to Horeb, the mount of God, fearful of retribution from Jezebel. There he sits, faithless and self-pitying, foolishly thinking that he is the only faithful prophet left in the land. In the very place where God spectacularly appeared to Moses and gave the law to Israel, the Lord again presents to Elijah the signs that traditionally accompanied his presence: earthquake, wind, and fire. Yet, Elijah is told that, on this occasion, God was not in these phenomena. Of course, God has sent them, but the Lord's point is that, on this occasion, they are not his vehicles of revelation. Then the prophet hears a low whisper. Although it is not made explicit, it is clear that Elijah rightly infers that God is present in the gentle, barely audible sound. However, this revelation makes absolutely no difference to the prophet, who remains just as dejected when he emerges from the cave.

What is the point of this revelation? Is the writer telling us that we ought to retreat to a cave-like place in order to encounter God in the silence? Of course not. Elijah had no right to be in that cave in the first place. He wasn't there on some spiritual sabbatical, seeking to have his batteries of faith recharged, ready to re-enter the fray against the forces of darkness. Far from it. His presence there was a testimony to his cowardice and faithlessness. He wasn't there to discern the voice of God. With the earthquake, wind, and fire, God's point is quite simply that he is not only present in his dramatic and spectacular actions, such as the one Elijah had witnessed on Mt Carmel. God is equally present and active when all appears still and quiet. In fact, the Lord goes on to remind Elijah that, unbeknown to him, there are seven thousand others (probably a symbolic figure meaning a large number), who have not compromised their spiritual integrity. Elijah may not have heard about them, and they may not have drawn attention to themselves, but they are there nonetheless, and so Elijah, despite his protestations, is not alone. The event that makes the difference to Elijah is not the sound of a whisper, but the word of God which follows it. It is then that the prophet gets his perspective realigned and sets out to meet Elisha (19:19ff).

Briefly, we also must make a comment about another verse which is just as abused and misused as 1 Kings 19. Psalm 46 describes God as the refuge and strength of his people in times of trouble. The psalmist reminds God's people of his unfailing presence among them and the fact that he is the one who triumphs over his enemies. Then in the midst of the strong affirmation that this God shatters the spear, this same awesome God speaks through his servant (actually I think he would thunder it out): "Be still, and know that I am God! I will be exalted among the nations" (v. 10). The image is akin to that of a teacher in the presence of an unruly class who bellows out: Sit down and shut up! I'm in charge here! The King of all creation is calling the world to attention and to recognize that in their midst stands the one "exalted in the earth". This isn't a call to wordlessness, understood as a spiritual discipline designed to bring you closer to God. It's a call to take on board the truth about this mighty God that has been proclaimed throughout the psalm, so that it might be a cause of unending comfort to those tossed and thrown about by the troubles of life and faith.

Contemplative prayer

Even more of a concern is the suggestion that a higher, or more intimate form of prayer is the prayer of few words, or even wordlessness. Described as 'contemplative prayer', the repetition of a biblical word or phrase (such as "Lord Jesus, have mercy") is said to create an inner stillness, so enabling the supplicant to listen to the voice of God. It is hard to think of anything more contrary to the spirit of prayer, and even the character of the believer's relationship to God.

Our brief survey of some of the mystical writings has shown that mysticism generally devalues language as an adequate means for apprehending the truth about God. There are serious flaws in this way of thinking. God created man and woman in his own image, and created them for relationship. At the heart of the relationship is verbal communication. This is what separates people from the rest of God's creation. God spoke to Adam. God made himself known to us in words. God finally revealed himself when the Word came amongst us. To argue that the less words we use, and ideally none at all, the closer we draw to God, cuts at the heart of the character of our relationship with God. With biblical wisdom and sober common sense, Ranald Macaulay and Jerram Barrs write,

> God is present with the believer and therefore the purpose of prayer in the scripture is to communicate to God in ordinary language one's praise, thanksgiving, confession, troubles and requests. Because God is personal and uses language himself, ordinary language is a perfectly good medium for communicating with God. God is not the absolute other. Language is not valueless to describe God, nor to speak to him.

Sometimes, of course, we may feel so troubled about a particular issue which faces us or so confused about how to pray in some situation that we cannot find words to express ourselves. Then the Spirit, who knows the deepest needs and desires of our hearts, prays for us.[7]

The essence of prayer is petition. Prayer is asking, and our problem, says Jesus, is that we don't ask enough. A failure to ask, and to continue to ask, is often not a mark of reluctance or humility, but pride. We don't ask because we think that we don't need. We don't need because we believe that we already have. It is often said that we should not bring our shopping list of requests to God. This is poor advice. The average Christian's problem is that their shopping list is far too short! Of course, our requests are to conform to God's will, but petition, along with thanksgiving, ought to be the hallmark of our prayer life. We can feel sometimes so full of a sense of our own adequacy and strength, that we can be tempted to believe that, in a given situation, we don't need divine aid. The point of prayer is that it is a continual acknowledgement of our childlike dependence on the Giver for everything. That is why petition is the verbal expression of faith. The endless repetition of a particular phrase may, after a time, give the petitioner a 'feeling' or a 'sense' of some presence, but it is not what biblical prayer is, and it bears no resemblance to the sort of prayers that Jesus and Paul modelled for us.

The essence of mysticism

We have already alluded to the fact that, for all the differences in the practices of piety and worship, mysticism shares a great deal in common with charismatic Christianity. Both mystics and charismatics testify to an experience of God, or the Spirit, which they feel has drawn them into a depth of relationship with God that they had not experienced before. This experience has revolutionized their Christian lives giving them the sense of a new power and effectiveness in ministry. This experience is then understood to be normative for all Christians, if they will only put the effort required into pursuing the presence of God that is required. Those who do not have it remain, somehow, just ordinary Christians, experiencing a lower level of intimacy with God. The means to achieve this higher Christian life is by following a series of procedures. Charismatic writings will suggest steps for speaking in tongues, or being filled with the Spirit, or receiving words of knowledge. Evangelical mystics like Bruce Demarest suggest various physical and mental exercises which will quieten the spirit, allow you to focus on God and, perhaps, experience his presence. Like charismatics, mystics do not promise that every experience of worship or meditation will result in sensing God's presence, but many will. In short, follow certain well-proven guidelines and God's presence is something you will know and feel, here and now. The alternative is to hold on to your theological prejudices, and remain a Christian who knows about God's power and presence, but for whom it remains little more than a textbook dogma which a person affirms, but has rarely experientially known.

But, whispers of Plato

While Christian mysticism first began to flower in the Egyptian desert, the medieval mystics explicitly and implicitly acknowledge their indebtedness to one of the ancient fathers of mysticism, the 5th-century philosopher Dionysius the Areopagite (also known as Pseudo-Dionysius, so-called because it is claimed that his writings are from the Dionysius converted by Paul in Athens [Acts 17:34]).

Dionysius' mysticism was essentially Platonic; or, to be more precise, neoplatonic. Although neoplatonism added many layers of complexity to Platonic thought, it retained with Plato the basic idea of the soul's ascent from the realm of illusion to an experience of the real. Building on, and interpreting, the writings of the philosophical giants, Plato and Aristotle, neoplatonism marked the final flowering of ancient Greek thought from the third to the sixth century A.D. The tentacles of its influence touched and influenced both Christian and Islamic thinking in the middle ages. It was the intellectual force behind the Italian Renaissance, and its influence was still being felt into the nineteenth century. Indeed, as we will see, its understanding of reality still lies behind a number of unquestioned assumptions about the nature of things that people, including Christians, make today.[8]

In Platonic thinking, reality comprises two separate and distinct parts. There is the material realm of the physical world. This is the realm of imperfection, appearances and shadows. The other realm is the spiritual. This is the superior realm of perfection, permanence and divinity. This is the realm of what Plato called forms and ideas. Plato did not mean by ideas 'human thought processes'. For him, ideas were the eternal, perfect forms or prototypes which have shadowy representations in the material world. For example, we talk of a beautiful flower or a beautiful sunset or a beautiful painting. We have the concept of beauty, of which these earthly things are shadowy reflections. However, Plato believed that in the spiritual world there was the perfect form, or idea, of beauty. This idea has its imperfect representation in the physical world in the shape of things like flowers and sunsets.

How did this Platonic perception of reality shape an understanding of the nature of the human being? As Plato divided reality into two parts, the (inferior) material and the (superior) spiritual, in the same way his understanding of people is *partitive*. That is, we are made up of distinct parts, what we call the material and the spiritual. The essential core of a person is the *psyche* or soul/life/mind, which can be separated from the body. The physical body is the home of the *psyche* . As the spiritual is superior to the material so the *psyche* is far more important than the body, and should be nourished and cared for, even at the expense of the body. The body is like a tomb or a prison, and the soul longs to be set free from its prison and fly back to the eternal world, which we have seen is the world of perfect forms.

This is the origin of the popular concept of the immortality of the soul. It is very common to hear Christians speak of death as that time when our body is left behind in the grave to waste away, while the 'real me', my soul or spirit, is whisked away to be with Christ. Many people think that once you die you enter a sphere of existence where you are without a body. You are now a kind of formless, vapour-like spirit floating and oozing across the ethereal cosmos. For Plato, while death will release the person from the realm of the physical, in the meantime people are to remain as much as possible in the spiritual realm. The spiritual is therefore elevated in people's thinking and the material is devalued.

It should be said from the outset that this partitive view of human beings stands in contrast to the way the Bible looks at people. The ancient Hebrews viewed people, not *partitively*, but *aspectively*. In other words, while the Bible talks about the body and mind, and soul and spirit, and you can speak of each one as a different *aspect* of the human personality, they can never really be separated. They are all part of the one, indivisible whole, the human being. New Testament scholar James Dunn helpfully illustrates the difference between a partitive and aspective view of people by saying that it is the difference between saying "The school has a gym", and saying "I am a Scot".[9] A gym is a part of a school, separate and distinct from it. Indeed, you could burn the school down and still leave the gym standing. However, being a Scot, or a father of three, or an introvert, or being short or tall, are all aspects of the one personality. You can talk about each aspect on its own, but if you strangle the Scot with his bagpipes then you destroy the whole person!

This has important implications for our life and behaviour. There is no immortal soul which is our essence, and which continues on into eternity, leaving the inferior, disposable rest of the person behind. The physical, psychological, intellectual, and emotional aspects of me are just as much an integral part of who I am as that aspect which we call the spiritual. In the next chapter we will look more closely at how the apostle Paul uses the terms 'spiritual' and 'unspiritual'. However, for the moment the point worth making is that the Bible doesn't break the human person up into separate and distinct parts. The resurrection hope for Christians is a hope for the resurrection of the whole person. We believe in a bodily resurrection. It is unthinkable for Paul that we will experience eternal life in some bodiless condition. To be human is to be embodied, and while our imperishable heavenly body will be more glorious and powerful than our perishable earthly body, there will be a clear continuity between the two (see 1 Cor 15:35-57).

Certainly, our resurrection body will be different from our earthly body, but the difference will not be one of matter and spirit. In 2 Corinthians 5 the metaphor Paul uses to illustrate the difference between the two is that of a building. The difference between our present bodily state and the one to come is akin to the difference between a tent and a building. Tents imply temporary accommodation. Indeed, the material used for a tent isn't all that durable. They are not designed for permanent occupation. That is how Paul views this earthly body. It's like camping in a tent.

But once this tent is destroyed God has waiting for us, already built and ready for immediate occupation, a lovely, strong, secure house. This is our heavenly body. There is no despising of the material in this image. Indeed, it may well be that Paul uses such concrete images in order to undermine any Platonic body/spirit dualism that might be influencing his readers' thinking about the resurrection.

Given this distinction between the material and the spiritual, neoplatonists understand knowledge to consist of a progression through degrees or levels to the highest level of comprehension. It is a movement from a lower level of understanding to a higher level. At the lower level one's mind is comprehending images or impressions of physical things. However, at the higher level one is comprehending the essence of things. For neoplatonists, the ultimate reality is that fundamental unity out of which we all came into being, and that is God himself. So, the purpose of knowledge is union with God, from which flows a state of wellbeing. The philosopher credited with being the founder of neoplatonism was

Plotinus (205-270). He was himself a mystic who claimed that on numerous occasions he experienced union with God or Ultimate Reality.

This knowledge of the perfect and the divine is obtained, or assimilated, through the soul. The soul is the avenue to union with God. Through contemplation and asceticism the soul can achieve a mystical return to the One from whom it emerged. The material realm has value only insofar as it can provide a trigger for the mystical contemplation of the sublime and spiritual. Macaulay and Barrs illustrate this with the example of a beautiful flower. I behold the beauty of a flower, but I don't remain contemplating its beauty. Rather, I see its beauty as imperfect, and I use this encounter as a sparkplug to ignite my contemplation of the true beauty of the world of the real which stands behind this world.[10] Therefore, concentrating on the soul involves a certain detachment from temporal, physical events.

The list of early Christian thinkers who were profoundly influenced by Plato and, later, neoplatonic thought is long and impressive. Justin Martyr went so far as to describe Plato as a Christian before Christ. Origen sought to discover the 'mystical sense' of scripture, by which he understood the hidden presence of Christ within the biblical text. Pseudo-Dionysius stressed the transcendence of God and the futility of language as a vehicle for making any meaningful statement about the one who is beyond all that exists. Rather, silence is the path to true union with God, since it is only in silence that one can come to a proper awareness of reality.

The impact of Platonic dualism on Christian thinking cannot be underestimated. We have already highlighted how common it is for Christians to divide the human being, such that the soul or spirit is thought of as a separate and superior entity. Far from such an understanding, the Bible esteems the body. We have just seen that our resurrection hope is not the destruction of an unwanted and cumbersome physical existence, but a transformation into an even richer and more wonderful physical life. To this can be added our propensity to separate the secular from the sacred. We place certain activities (prayer, Bible study, fellowship) in the separate and superior category of the sacred, while the rest of life is reduced to that which is "just secular". In the scriptures, though, everything we do can be done, and is to be done, for the glory of God. We divide God's gifts to his people into the categories of the natural (the lower level gifts like administration and helps) and the supernatural (or higher level gifts like healing and prophecy) when the Bible uses the terms *charismata* (gifts of grace) or *pneumatika* (gifts of the Spirit) to cover the whole range of God's gifts to his people (see Rom 12:6-8, 1 Cor 12).

From this very brief overview of Platonic thought, the extent of the influence of this philosophy on the writings of the ancient and medieval mystics, in particular, is readily obvious. The perception that God cannot properly be known through the mind, but rather through the spirit, leads to a devaluing of reason and human language, the devaluing of the body, and the elevation of extraordinary spiritual or ecstatic experiences. Such beliefs created the idea that the purpose of spirituality is subjective union with God. In short, it is crucial to bear in mind that when one traces the river of mysticism back to its source, one finds oneself in the thought world of this ancient pagan Greek philosopher.

But, don't we have the presence of God?

According to the mystical way, the presence of God is something that a person ought to strive to experience. According to scripture it is a reality which, by faith, every believer already does experience. "And behold, I am with you always", said the Lord Jesus. Certainly, our great hope as Christians is that one day we will see him face to face, but in the meantime all those who have put their faith in Christ receive the Holy Spirit who is God with us. The fact that Christ is in, and with, every Christian, is an assumed premise of the teaching of the New Testament (Gal 2:20, 2 Cor 13:5). It is pastorally destructive to suggest that the presence of God (or the power of the Spirit of God) is some other/extra/later experience a believer should seek. In Christ, all his children have been blessed with every spiritual blessing which he longs to give them, and these blessings are appropriated by faith in the crucified and risen Saviour.

Further, it is unhelpful to suggest that certain techniques or practices can elevate Christians to a different level of Christian being. This was the great error that the church in Colossae faced, and that Paul warned against. The precise nature of the Colossian heresy is still debated, although Peter O'Brien argues that it appears to have been related to some form of Jewish asceticism and mysticism, which offered spiritual 'fullness' through following certain ascetic techniques which were effective for receiving visions of heavenly mysteries and participating in mystical experiences.[11] Paul's attack on these false teachers was devastating. In short, he says that all who have been incorporated into Christ have fullness of life in him (2:10). Paul writes to the church:

Let no one disqualify you, insisting on asceticism and

worship of angels, going on in detail about visions, puffed up without reason by his sensuous mind, and not holding fast to the Head, from whom the whole body, nourished and knit together through its joints and ligaments, grows with a growth that is from God (2:18-19).

The believers in Colossae lack nothing of the power of God's presence. There are no elite Christians who have gone higher or deeper into spiritual truths or experiences. In Christ is the totality of wisdom and knowledge.

So much of contemporary spirituality is about discovering the eternal truths that are within you. It is not surprising, then, that much of the appeal of mysticism lies in the fact that it is a spirituality of the inner person. Brother Lawrence advises the reader to worship God inwardly. Since God abides "at the very depth and centre of your soul" (p. 112), then we ought to withdraw within ourselves to worship him. In the same vein, Teresa of Avila tells us that the treasure of union with God "lies within our very selves" (p.86). For Bruce Demarest "nurturing the inner man" should be a major concern of each Christian. Richard Foster, who has probably done more to commend the mystical way to evangelicals than anyone else in recent times, emphasizes the centrality of the spiritual journey inwards. He writes,

> If we hope to move beyond the superficialities of our culture ... we must be willing to go down into the recreating silences, into the inner world of contemplation.[12]

But is this inward journey in pursuit of the presence of God what the Bible calls us to? The goal of the Christian life is conformity to the image of Christ. It is to this good end that God sovereignly works the events our life (Rom 8:28), and it is to this goal that he gives gifts to his church (Eph 4:9-13). Certainly, the Bible calls us to focus on Christ, but not the Christ within. We are to seek the things that are above, where Christ is (Col 3:1ff). Christ as Lord reigns in heaven and, by faith, we are united with him there. Our focus, therefore, ought to be on this reality. Rather than disparaging our minds, Paul then says that the fact of our heavenly union with Christ will lead us to "set our minds on things that are above", not on a life within. The consequence of this will be, not a vision, or a sense of his presence, but godly, moral conduct (3:5ff). Lewis Smedes sums up the Pauline teaching on faith and union with Christ succinctly and incisively:

> In a sense, we are not aware of Christ within at all. We do not feel, or intuit, or sense His presence as something distinct from ourselves. We are not summoned by the gospel to believe that he is within; we are summoned by faith in the Christ of the cross and resurrection. Nor are we urged to investigate our inner lives to discover Christ there; the test is in the effects of the Spirit and the power in our moral lives.[13]

In their hunger for something more, Christians will always be attracted to those who sympathetically say, "I know how you feel. I was once where you are now. I, too, thought that just believing in Jesus and serving him as Lord was enough and that's all there is. But let me tell you, that's not all there is. Much more is available. All you have to do is ... (fill in the blank)". This is the lure of mysticism.

The biblical facts are that we don't journey inwards. There

are no spiritual elites. We don't have to strive for the presence of God. Christians *are* fully one with God. Our God is both love and a consuming fire. God communicates essentially in words. The believer's mind is not to be emptied of thoughts, but filled with right thoughts about God and Christ.

But we are running ahead of ourselves. What, in fact, does the Bible have to say about spirituality? What does a spiritual man or woman look like? Does it address the question of the undeniable thirst that God's people feel for a deeper encounter with him? Can we grow 'spiritually' as Christians, without compromising biblical truth and falling into some of the theological pitfalls that elitist spiritualities have set? It is to this question that we now turn.

ENDNOTES

1   Arthur Paul Boers, 'Learning the ancient rhythms of prayer', *Christianity Today*, January 8th, 2001.

2   The similarities between mysticism and contemporary Christianity are immediately obvious. In fact, Arthur Johnson, in his book, *Faith Misguided: Exposing the Dangers of Mysticism* (Moody Press, Chicago, 1988) describes the charismatic movement as the zenith of mysticism. One can trace a direct line between the mystics and the pentecostal/charismatic movements of the twentieth-century. The mystics influenced men like William Law (*A Serious Call to a Devout and Holy Life*) and John Wesley (fifty-volume, *The Christian Library*) whose writings themselves, in turn, influenced the mystically-inclined 'holiness' movement and Keswick movements of the nineteenth century. The modern pentecostal and charismatic movement is the spiritual offspring of these holiness movements.

3   Tommy Tenney, *The God Catchers: Experiencing the Manifest Presence of God*, Thomas Nelson, Nashville, 2000, p. 51.

4   Demarest, *Satisfy Your Soul*, p. 25.

5   Demarest, *Satisfy Your Soul*, p. 119 (Demarest here is quoting AW Tozer).

6   Norris, *The Cloister Walk*, p. 14.

7   Ranald Macaulay and Jerram Barrs, *Being Human: The Nature of Spiritual Experience*, IVP, Downers Grove, 1978, p. 58.

8   I am indebted to the excellent articles on Platonism and neoplatonism in Edward Craig (ed.), *Encyclopaedia of Philosophy*, Routledge, London and New York, 1998. See also WKC Guthrie, *The Greek Philosophers: from Thales to Aristotle*, Methuen, London, 1950, chapter V. There is also a very fine analysis of the influence of Platonic thought on mysticism in Macaulay and Barrs, *Being Human*, pp. 38-59.

9   James DG Dunn, *The Theology of Paul the Apostle*, Eerdmans, Grand Rapids, 1998, p. 54.

10 Macaulay and Barrs, *Being Human*, pp. 40-41.

11 Peter O'Brien, *Understanding the Basic Themes of Colossians, Philemon*, Word, Waco, 1991, p. 6.

12 Richard Foster, *Celebration of Discipline: the Path to Spiritual Growth* (rev. ed.), Harper & Row, San Francisco, 1988, p. 15.

13 Lewis Smedes, *Union with Christ: A Biblical View of New Life in Christ*, Eerdmans, Grand Rapids, 1983, p. 156.

Chapter 8

True Spirituality: Listening to the Apostle of the Spirit

WE HAVE TAKEN, so far, a bird's eye view of the new spirituality. We've swept over the phenomenon and, hopefully, seen something of both its size and shape. We've just finished a closer analysis of one particular type of popular spirituality, and that is mysticism. Indeed, so much of modern spirituality is really mystical in its essence. Hopefully we now have a better idea of what people mean when they bandy around the term 'spirituality'. We've also seen that some Christian expressions of spirituality advocate ways of relating to God that appear to be a departure from how the Lord himself has told us we should relate to him. More seriously, some of these movements, while promising us a greater intimacy with God, may actually undermine the very gospel we have received which is the power of our salvation. While we have also examined Paul's analysis and critique of some of the 'spiritualities' of his own day, we still haven't yet looked at what the Bible has to say about the character of true spirituality.

Depending on how you biblically define the term 'spirituality', this could be an enormous topic. If you were to define it, say, as 'the way or ways of relating to God' then the whole of the Bible deals with this issue. One would have to start with man and woman in the Garden of Eden and follow a long investigation right through the scriptures until the end, when we would examine man and woman in the new Eden. It would be difficult to see how such an investigation wouldn't take in every part of the believer's life.

The problem might be solved if we just turned up our concordance and looked under the word 'spirituality'. Well, it may not surprise you to learn that the term 'spirituality' does not, in fact, appear in any concordance of the Bible. It's not a word the Bible uses. However, all is not lost. The adjective 'spiritual' does appear on a number of occasions and, with only one exception, they are all in the writings of Paul.[1] This isn't surprising, given that Paul has rightly been dubbed 'the apostle of the Spirit'.

When Paul writes of spiritual things, he mentions spiritual gifts, spiritual songs, spiritual sacrifices. The law of Moses is spiritual. In each case, the spirit referred to is the divine Spirit. When Paul describes the law as spiritual, he is referring to its divine origin. Spiritual gifts are gifts distributed by the Spirit. Spiritual songs are songs prompted by the Spirit. Similarly, when Paul speaks of people as 'spiritual', he is not referring to people for whom a constituent part of their personhood is a spirit, which seeks some transcendent connection. We have already seen that if we are using 'spirit' this way—in a way that implies that the soul or spirit is a distinct part of the human person—then this is an anthropology that is foreign to the Bible. When Paul describes people as spiritual he is talking about people indwelt by, and energized by, the Spirit of God.

In other words, when we turn to look at what the Bible, and the apostle Paul in particular, has to say about spirituality, it becomes immediately obvious that the focus is not anthropocentric. That is, Paul is not describing the activity or nurture of the human spirit. Paul's thinking is theocentric, that is, he is focussing on the work of God's Spirit in people's lives. Christian spirituality, then, is the study of the work of the Holy Spirit in the life of the believer. James Dunn writes, "for Paul the gospel is not about an innate spirituality awaiting release, but about the divine Spirit acting upon a person from without."[2]

Spiritual men and women

Let's begin by looking at Paul's description of people as spiritual beings. From the outset, it is clear that, for the apostle Paul, the term 'spiritual' cannot apply to every human being. In 1 Corinthians 2:14ff, he contrasts two kinds of people: the spiritual (*pneumatikos*) and the natural or unspiritual (*psychikos*). The latter term, *psychikos*, is derived from the word *psyche*, which we have already noted is often translated 'soul'. The soul in the New Testament is generally just a term for life, or personhood. Jesus says that "whoever would save his life (*psyche*) will lose it" (Mark 8:35), and when Paul is shipwrecked, there were 276 souls on the ship (Acts 27:37).

However, when the adjective *psychikos* is used, it is always in a negative sense of being worldly, earthly, devoid of the Spirit of God. According to James, selfish ambition is earthly, unspiritual (*psychike*), and demonic (3:15). Standing opposite the unspiritual or 'soulful' person is the spiritual man or woman, the person possessed by the Spirit of God, and who exhibits the mark of the presence of the Spirit in his or her life.

In summary, being spiritual in the New Testament is being indwelt by the Spirit of God. Only those people so indwelt can, biblically, be described as spiritual. Spirituality, then, is the expression or manifestation in a person's life of the indwelling of the Spirit. But are all Christians spiritual? Are some Christians more spiritual than others? Is there a higher level of spirituality to which we must strive, and which some attain?

In chapter 2 of 1 Corinthians, Paul says that the human race is divided into those people who are spiritual and those who are not. However, in the following chapter he seems to suggest that only some Christians deserve the epithet 'spiritual', while others, while converted, are carnal. The apostle writes,

> But I, brothers, could not address you as spiritual people, but as people of the flesh, as infants in Christ. I fed you with milk, not solid food, for you were not ready for it. And even now you are not yet ready, for you are still of the flesh. For while there is jealousy and strife among you, are you not of the flesh and behaving only in a human way? (3:1-3)

The very fact that Paul begins this section with the word 'brothers', indicates that now he is referring to Christians. A Christian, by definition, is someone who has the Spirit (Rom 8:9); if anyone does not have the Spirit this person does not belong to God. Yet Paul describes at least some amongst the Corinthian believers as not being spiritual, but being worldly, or fleshly. Are there, then, two categories of Christian? The carnal Christian, who has the Spirit, but who could not really be described as being 'spiritual', and the higher, more spiritual Christian? Is there, in actual fact, an elitism in the Christian community after all?

The answer appears to be 'no' ... and 'yes'! Why does Paul identify some of these believers as fleshly? It is because they are still manifesting the works of the flesh in their lives, in particular jealousy and quarrelling. It is not that they are just, from time to time, slipping back into some old bad habits, but that they are continually behaving as if they have never been converted. This is all despite the fact that they had received the Spirit of God. Paul finds such behaviour absolutely incongruous, all the more so given the fact that they have now been believers for some time.

In short, it was Paul's expectation that once someone was converted and had received the Spirit of God, then there would immediately be some transformation in their behaviour. There is no reason why a person, from the moment of regeneration, should not be controlled by the Spirit who now dwells within them, and surrender to his control. In other words, Paul's expectation is that, from the moment of conversion, God's people ought to be spiritual. Spiritual means to be 'of the Spirit', and that means to be controlled by the Spirit. Such a person is one, in Paul's own terms, who walks by the Spirit (Gal 5:16). This submission to the Spirit is evidenced in one's behaviour. However, the reality is that while Christians are indwelt by the Spirit, they still remain in the flesh. That's why in every letter Paul wrote he had to persistently exhort his readers to godly conduct. All these exhortations address the ongoing problem that every Christian faces, of a struggle between the desires of the Spirit and the inclinations of the flesh. Galatians 5 is the most detailed and explicit account of this struggle. It is clear that some Christians surrender themselves more to the control of the Spirit, and do not allow the flesh to dominate their thinking and conduct. Other Christians are less committed to the battle or, for a variety of reasons, find the flesh exercising more control over them than they would wish. Some in the Corinthian church appear to have given up on this battle altogether, such that, on the evidence of their conduct, they appear to be little different from the unconverted pagans around them. When they behave in such a way, Paul simply cannot describe such people as spiritual. And should they continue the way they are, then he will not be able to even describe them as Christian!

Let's summarize. Firstly, for Paul to be spiritual is to walk by the Spirit, which means to have the Spirit of God controlling your thoughts, attitudes, and behaviour. Secondly, this is the normal Christian life. Paul expects every Christian to be spiritual, and to behave in a way consistent with what, by God's grace, he or she has become. Because every Christian is in the Spirit, he or she will live by the Spirit. Thirdly, because we still have a sinful flesh, all Christians sometimes, and some Christians far too much of the time, behave in a carnal or unspiritual way. The remedy for this is repentance, and to live by the Spirit again. Indeed, when a believer surrenders to the flesh, Paul enjoins "those who are spiritual", that is the other believers in the body, to gently restore him (Gal 6:1). The "spiritual ones" here are not some elite, super-spiritual group in the congregation, but ordinary Christians who are keeping in step with the Spirit.

Christian spirituality

Christian spirituality is a term we can use to describe the character of the life of those people who are truly spiritual. Let us now turn again to the great theologian of the Spirit, Paul, and briefly examine what he has to say about the spiritual life. We will look at just three key passages which speak about life in the Spirit, but also draw in reflections from other parts of the New Testament. By starting with scripture and letting God's word inform our understanding, we are less likely to define spirituality in terms of our own preconceptions of what it should be like.

Romans 8

This 'mountain peak' of scripture is rightly understood as the Bible's most extensive treatment on the work of the Spirit. Our purpose here is not an extensive survey of Paul's teaching on the person and work of the Spirit, but only to look at the characteristics of the life of someone led by the Spirit.

Paul begins by summarising the great truth that he has been arguing since the beginning of chapter 5: that there is no condemnation for those in Christ Jesus. We see here the triune God active in this work of salvation. God the Father has sent the Son who, by his atoning death, has dealt with the problem of sin, and on the basis of this the Spirit sets us free and empowers those who walk according to the Spirit to fulfil the righteous requirement of the law (8:4). This 'righteous requirement' is the obedience of faith (1:5), the good work (2:7) which Paul has already referred to in this letter. What the law could not achieve in the lives of God's people, Christ has achieved by his death and resurrection. The outworking of Jesus' death is that his people now have the Spirit. Paul says that the law's righteous requirement is fulfilled in those who "walk in the Spirit" (which is Paul's shorthand way of saying those who conduct their lives in a way pleasing to God), suggesting that Paul sees this manner of life as the fulfilment of the obligation that the law had placed before people.[3]

Paul then goes on to say that spiritual people set their minds on spiritual things (vv. 5-7). There is a radical difference here between those who are ruled by the flesh, and those who live under the influence of the Spirit. These are two completely different realms of existence. In one realm are those who set their minds on the flesh, that is, those whose entire life orientation is away from God and focussed on self. In marked contrast to such people are those who live and move in the sphere of the Spirit, those whose thinking, and thus whose way of living, is controlled by the Spirit. The consequence of a life focussed on the flesh is death, but the Spirit-controlled mind issues in life and peace. Against mystics who wish to denigrate the mind as an inadequate vehicle for comprehending spiritual truth, Paul sees a renewed mind as the essential starting point for living the spiritual life. Indeed, one is to continually renew one's mind so that one can discern the will of God (Rom 12:2).

The relationship between life in the Spirit and personal holiness is reiterated in verses 12-13. Paul's point is simply that, since we are in the Spirit, we have an obligation to live accordingly and this involves putting to death the deeds of the body. Life in the Spirit is a life which pursues righteousness and rejects sin.

In the next section of the chapter, Paul's emphasis shifts from what the Spirit causes us to do, to what the Spirit testifies we are. He writes that "all who are led by the Spirit of God are sons of God" (v. 14). To be led by God's Spirit is not a reference to some ecstatic or mystical experience, or even some sense of divine guidance for one's life. The background is the Old Testament, where in a variety of ways God is said to lead his people "in paths of righteousness, for his name's sake". God's Spirit leads God's people in the ways of God, and in so doing, demonstrates that they are the sons of God.[4] What is more, this same Spirit both bestows on us the privilege of adoption as God's children, and confirms in us that this is what we really are. When we cry out "Abba, Father", it is a cry we make in the Spirit (v. 15). For any Christian this must be a deeply moving experience. Douglas Moo comments,

> Paul stresses that our awareness of God as Father comes not from rational consideration nor from external testimony alone but from a truth deeply felt and intensely experienced. If some Christians err in basing their assurance of salvation on feelings alone,

many others err in basing it on facts and arguments alone. Indeed, what Paul says here calls into question whether one can have a genuine experience of God's Spirit of adoption without its affecting the emotions.[5]

The experiential dimension of our life in the Spirit continues in the next section, where Paul speaks of our weaknesses. Along with the rest of creation, believers groan in travail, as they await the final redemption of their bodies. The Spirit we now experience is really just the first fruits of the full reality that awaits us when the end comes. For the writers of the Bible, the coming of the Spirit was an end-time event, marking the consummation of all things. Although the end has not yet finally come, we experience now something of the reality of that future. The Spirit is a foretaste of that. Yet it is not the full experience; and, in the meantime, we live and groan with that frustration. However, the Spirit is not only our guarantee that we belong to the age to come, he also, right here and now, helps us in our weaknesses by praying to God on our behalf "with groanings too deep for words" (v. 26). Part of our frustration is that, in a world of suffering and rampant human evil, where we only see "in a mirror dimly", we often do not know what to pray. We do not know God's perfect will in a given situation. This adds to our sense of frustration. At times like this the Spirit intercedes for us before the Father. Paul metaphorically describes these prayers of the Spirit as inaudible groans. They express perfectly to God what, because of our weakness, we could never discern, nor properly put into words. Even more thrilling is the confidence that these prayers are heard and answered because God knows the mind of the Spirit.

Romans 8 and Christian spirituality

Before moving on, it might be helpful just to draw a few conclusions about the character of spirituality in the light of this important passage of scripture.

Firstly, the spiritual life is intimately related to the saving work of God in Christ. Here in Romans 8, and elsewhere in the New Testament, Paul bases his teaching on life in the Spirit on the work of Christ. He regularly links the work of the Spirit with the atoning work of Christ. The Christian has died and risen with Christ and now this same Christ lives in the believer by his Spirit. This Spirit then enables the believer to live a Christ-like life, working to transform him into the likeness of his Lord. What all this means is that we cannot discuss spirituality apart from the saving work of Christ. Any spiritual 'classic' that is silent about the work of Christ, or does not understand this work as central to its understanding of the presence of God, is woefully wide of the mark.

Secondly, for Paul, spirituality, or life in the Spirit, was much more about living a life of righteousness, than performing personal and private acts of devotion. Spirituality is concerned, fundamentally, with fulfilling the will of God, which is loving God with all your heart, soul, and mind, and loving your neighbour as yourself. Contemporary spirituality is about the freedom to express yourself in any way you want. The Other that people seek connection with in today's spiritualities, is an Other who places few limits on behaviour, and refuses to condemn or restrict. This, though, is the antithesis of true spirituality. Life in the Spirit is a life that wages war against selfishness and sin. It is a life that pursues holiness and righteousness.

Thirdly, Christian spirituality recognizes the importance of the mind in pursuing a life pleasing to God. Elsewhere Paul writes, "Have this mind among yourselves, which is yours in Christ Jesus" (Phil 2:5), and, "Set your minds on things that are above" (Col 3:2). In each case, the exhortation to right thinking is not for the accumulation of knowledge for accumulation sake, but in order to live a godly life, a life of humility and goodness. There is nothing dry and cerebral about this kind of spirituality. This is not to say that people cannot reduce spirituality to something merely academic, and end up with a form of Christianity that rarely touches the heart or motivates the will. However, equally as dangerous is a spirituality that denigrates the mind, or suggests that there is a way to deeper intimacy with God, and conformity to his character, that bypasses the mind.

Fourthly, there is a deeply personal dimension to an encounter with the Spirit of God. Paul isolates one dimension of this here: the awareness, which is both objective and subjective, that God is our Father, and that we are intimately related to him. In her book, *I Dared to Call Him Father,* Muslim convert Bilquis Sheikh describes her conversion, and the understanding given to her that the God of Jesus Christ in whom she now believed, was her heavenly Father:

> "Oh Father, my Father ... Father God". Hesitantly, I spoke his name aloud. I tried different ways of speaking to Him. And then, as if something broke through for me I found myself trusting that He was indeed hearing me, just as my earthly father had always done. "Father, oh my Father God", I cried, with growing confidence. My voice seemed unusually loud

in the large bedroom as I knelt on the rug beside my bed. But suddenly that room wasn't empty any more. *He* was there!⁶

While Bilquis had been told that Christians addressed God as 'Father', her certainty that he was *her* Father was a truth that the Spirit testified to her. The passion of her words reflect, rightly, the wonder of this spiritual experience. Indeed, it is striking that Muslims, who find the concept of a triune God to be an absolute anathema, so often upon conversion know instinctively that God is Father, Son and Spirit. From the moment of new birth they begin to address God naturally and comfortably as 'Father'. This is much more than the exchanging of one set of theological formulae for a new set. It is much more than "Allah the merciful and omniscient", becoming "the God and Father of our Lord Jesus Christ". It is a realization of an intimacy with God that they had never experienced before. It is a certain assurance that this God who has forgiven, accepted, and adopted them, will also glorify them with his Son, Jesus Christ.

Fifthly, suffering is the context in which Christian spirituality is lived out. Paul tells us that in our weakness, the Spirit helps us to pray. When Paul speaks of suffering here he is referring to the whole gamut of human misery and pain. This includes, but is not limited to, those sufferings that believers endure for the sake of Christ. A life of suffering, then, is the context in which we experience the help and empowering of the Spirit. Indeed, one can even say that there can be no spiritual growth, no maturing as a believer, apart from suffering.

In Philippians 3:10 Paul writes of his hope "that I may know Christ and the power of his resurrection, and may share his sufferings, becoming like him in his death". The desire of those who long for a deeper spirituality is that they might gain a more intimate and experiential knowledge of Christ, to the degree that they become conscious of his presence. Here in this passage, Paul directly addresses this concern, and gives us the path to growth in a relationship with Jesus. Surprisingly, though, it is a path that few who write on mysticism, or indeed on Christian discipleship generally, choose to mention, and even fewer seek to walk.

Paul has already spoken of the incomparable worth of knowing Christ personally (Phil 3:8), but now he expresses the desire to know him even more fully. This will be achieved as he knows experientially both power and suffering. In fact, these two go hand in hand, as it is the power of Christ's risen life that enables Paul to persevere in these sufferings. Since it is the sufferings of Christ that are in view here, Paul must be referring to those hardships, anxieties, and persecutions that result from his life of obedience and service to his master. As he endures them for Jesus' sake, he is in fellowship with his Master who walked the path of suffering before him. Indeed, experiencing Christ's risen power in and through these sufferings actually works to deepen his knowledge of his Saviour.

Contemporary writers who give advice on pursuing the presence of God regularly provide techniques which can orchestrate a sense of his presence. One advocate writes that the principles and laws governing his presence are constant, and all we need to do is "get hot enough" and "create the atmosphere" that will enable us to catch his presence. I've no doubt the atmosphere was pretty hot when Paul stood before those who sought to kill him for his faith. And I suspect that the atmosphere was also hot as Paul confronted those in his churches who were turning people away from the cross of Christ to other more appealing gospels. Yet, I'm sure that these are not the sort of 'hot atmospheres' that most modern-day purveyors of spiritual experiences have in mind. In the ready-to-order consumer society, spirituality is 'on tap', cheap, and available for one's personal satisfaction. In the kingdom of God, though, the path to genuine depth of intimacy with Jesus Christ is found by walking the road of suffering which he walked.

In 1991 my brother-in-law, Joel, spent six months as a captive of a local commander of the *mujahideen* in Afghanistan. Cut off from family and friends, often in isolation, and for much of the time without a Bible, Joel faced each day uncertain whether it would hold the promise of release, or death. Joel has given much of his life to serving the various people groups of that part of the world, and now, for Christ's sake, he was suffering at the hands of a greedy and unscrupulous local leader. It is a kind of suffering that few of us could even contemplate, let alone feel we could endure. Through the entire experience Joel kept a diary. At the end of the diary he wrote, "My ordeal here has been agonizing, yes, but not without blessings. When I think of these, I am overwhelmed". The next 15 pages of the book is a catalogue of the blessings God has brought to him through this ordeal. He mentions that he learnt to pray without growing weary, to wait on God and develop patience, to re-evaluate his understanding of concepts like 'time well spent' and 'time wasted', and to know in a deeper and more profound way the unfailing goodness of God. To meet Joel is to meet a man who knows the Lord Jesus, and the maturity of this personal knowledge has been deepened through his experiences of suffering.[7]

Sixthly, frustration will be one aspect of life in the Spirit for each and every believer. Much of contemporary spirituality promises the complete satisfaction of all our spiritual and physical desires. We have seen that many New Age spiritualities purport to offer, through some spiritual connection, everything from peace and happiness, to material prosperity and a cure for AIDS. Some mystics claim that, here and now, we can enter into the heavenly experience of meeting God. We can have such a sense of his presence that we have entered, in Teresa of Avila's words, into the dwelling place of the Most Blessed Trinity, into "another heaven".

All of these desires, from the longing for a perfect encounter with God, to the freedom from sickness and anxiety, are perfectly natural. They are expressions of the desire for 'eternity' that, as we have already seen, God has put into our hearts. Yet this gift of a divine awareness is matched by the judgement of frustration that these longings can never be fully satisfied. The writer of Ecclesiastes describes this frustration as a sense of the futility or emptiness or meaninglessness of life. The word is *hebel*, which means 'breath', 'vapour', 'mist', 'transience'. For the Teacher, *hebel* is a defining element of life in this world. Wherever he turns, the writer finds each and every dimension of life permeated by a sense of *hebel*. Certainly, through the gospel, Christians have had much more revealed to them about God and life than the Teacher had. He knew nothing of the suffering Messiah. He would have had only the vaguest notion of the resurrection of the dead. He certainly could not have imagined the wonderful apocalypse that was revealed to the apostle John, and then recorded for our edification. So we will temper many of his sober reflections in the light of the gospel of Jesus. However, he gives us a perspective on life that we neglect to our great spiritual detriment.

It is striking how regularly Christian commentators on Ecclesiastes try to avoid some of the, quite frankly, depressing conclusions about life that this biblical book forces us to confront. For example, Bruce Demarest argues that Ecclesiastes presents us with a depressing picture of the disappointments of life *for those whose lives are not centred on God and lived in communion with him* (italics mine). He then concludes, that, "Fortunately the Teacher does not leave us despairing. In God our hearts find satisfaction and meaning".[8] For those who have turned to God in Christ, there is the answer to the despairing view of life which Ecclesiastes describes. In support of this, Demarest directs us to Ecclesiastes 2:24-26, which speaks of God giving joy to those who please him: "for apart from him who can eat or who can have enjoyment".

Yet this is a most superficial reading of the passage, for even in these verses the Teacher cannot allow this apparently more optimistic note to go unchallenged and unqualified. He again concludes, "this also is vanity and a striving after the wind" (2:26). This is the refrain that runs through the whole book. In other words, even in finding satisfaction in God there is still, says the Teacher, the pervasive presence of *hebel*. The Teacher's point is that life is full of disappointments, frustrations, and conundrums, both for those whose lives are centred on God, and for those whose lives are godless.

Paul picks up this theme in Romans 8. The futility that the whole created order has been subjected to is that same sense of weary frustration that the ancient Teacher became so aware of in his survey of the human condition. However, while acknowledging the rightness of Ecclesiastes' diagnosis, Paul's prognosis is different. Because of the gospel, he understands that this subjection to frustration is a subjection *in hope*. Groaning and disappointment is not the end of the story. The end is the certain and glorious liberation of the sons of God. However, while we await this redemption we, along with the whole created order, must live with the frustration. Frustration is not the whole story, but it is a dominant thread and runs through all of life, human and subhuman, Christian and non-Christian.

It is this important perspective on life generally, and life in the Spirit in particular, that is missing in so much teaching on spirituality. That God's people are hungry and thirsty for 'something more' in their spiritual lives is right and natural. And, indeed, it may be that the teaching they have been given on life in the Spirit has only served to heighten their sense of being dry and parched. However to suggest, as some do, that complete satisfaction can be found here and now is both unbiblical and, pastorally, very unhelpful. Paul asks, "who hopes for what he sees?" (Rom 8:24). Similarly, one could ask, who longs for what can be fully experienced now? If here and now we have entered into "the portal of privileged access enjoyed only by true worshippers", and found the keys "to unlock the heavens" (Tommy Tenney) then there is little left to hope for. The paradox of spirituality is that Christ, by his Spirit, satisfies our thirst, but never to the extent that we don't long to come back for more. As long as we live in the 'not yet' of this age, we will thirst for more of the living water. We will groan at the frustration of this. But we must turn our ears away from those who promise to finally quench that thirst and quell that groaning here and now.

Galatians 5

In Galatians 5 Paul describes what a spiritual life will look like. In verse 16 he presents what is really the foundational imperative of his entire ethical system: walk by the Spirit. While love is the first and great commandment, the fulfilling of this commandment is only possible as people walk by the Spirit. The command to walk by the Spirit is an imperative to keep on doing it. It is not something we do from time to time, but it ought to be the believer's ongoing experience and activity. The result of such a life is that the desire of the flesh will not be gratified.

Paul then describes the outward manifestation of such a spiritual life. He lists some of the fruit of the Spirit. This is not a complete list (indeed, this is made clear by his term "such things", implying there are others), but it is representative. Again we see an emphasis on good behaviour towards others, with virtues such as love, patience (towards others), and kindness. However, that does not exhaust the extent of Paul's spirituality here. Joy is a fruit of the spirit. There is the joy of knowing the amazing grace of God. The joy of being part of a community committed to one another in love. The joy of knowing a Father who is working all things together for good in our lives. Peace also marks the life of the spiritual man or woman. Given that the works of the flesh describe a community life marked by discord and disharmony (jealousy, anger, quarrels, dissension, envy), then at the forefront of the peace which the Spirit works in our lives is peaceful relationships. Of course, this communal peace results from the peace we enjoy through our reconciliation with God through Jesus Christ.

Chapter 5 of Galatians ends with the exhortation, "If we live by the Spirit, let us also walk by the Spirit" (v. 25), and Paul then practically shows how this will display itself in the life of the church: "Let us not become conceited, provoking one another, envying one another" (v. 26). While this is undoubtedly addressing a particular problem that the Galatian congregation was facing, yet again we see that the immediate outworking of true spirituality is in the context of our human relationships. How incongruous, then, that for so many people the place for the development of spirituality is the lonely desert. They tell us that it is in solitude that a person can experience the filling of the Spirit and the presence of God. While there is a time to 'get away', and recharge one's batteries, again and again for Paul the practice of spirituality takes place in the ongoing, everyday context of human relationships.

Ephesians 5

A discussion of the spirituality of Paul would be incomplete without a few comments on his command to the Ephesian Christians—and therefore, to us—to be filled by the Spirit. The apostle writes,

> Do not get drunk with wine, for that is debauchery,
> but be filled with the Spirit,
> *addressing* each other in psalms and hymns and
> spiritual songs,
> *singing* and *making melody* to the Lord with all
> your heart,
> *giving thanks* always and for everything to God the
> Father in the name of our Lord Jesus Christ,
> *submitting* to one another out of reverence for Christ
> (5:18-21).

The primary command in the passage is "be filled by (or with) the Spirit". This important expression is normally translated "with the Spirit", indicating that the content of the filling is the Holy Spirit. However, syntactically, this would be very unusual and, more importantly, on every other occasion in the epistle, when Paul uses the fullness language, it refers to God or Jesus. In 1:23, the church shares the fullness of Jesus who fills all things. In 3:19, Paul prays that we might be filled with all the fullness of God. In 4:10, Jesus, again, is said to fill all things. And in 4:13, the goal of ministry in the church is that believers might be mature, which is that they might attain the fullness of Christ.

In the light of this, it is likely that what Paul means by this phrase is that the Holy Spirit mediates the fullness of God and Christ to believers.[9] In other words, the Spirit is to continually transform God's people so that they are changed more and more into the image of Christ. Again, as we saw earlier, there is a strong ethical and behavioural dimension to Pauline spirituality. This is borne out by Paul's graphic contrast between being filled with Jesus, and being drunk with wine. The latter is a work of the flesh that Christians are to renounce. Just as it is immediately obvious that someone has had too much to drink by the way they talk, walk, and behave generally, so it should be immediately obvious to observers that a community of people are filled with all the fullness of Christ by the way they talk and conduct themselves.

By means of five participles which then follow (addressing, singing, making melody, giving thanks, submitting) Paul describes the character of such a Spirit-filled community. Firstly, it is a community marked by singing. Addressing, singing and making melody here all refer to the same activity. By the same token we do not need to draw hard and fast distinctions between psalms, hymns, and spiritual songs. However, it is worth noting two things. Singing has always been a mark of the community of faith. From the song of Moses which the redeemed people of Israel sang spontaneously after their deliverance through the Red Sea, to the song of Moses and the Lamb which the victorious saints sing in heaven, God's people have always responded to the gift of salvation with praise. There would be something utterly incongruous about a Christian congregation for which joyful singing was not a regular feature of their gatherings. Secondly, this singing has two foci. Firstly, the community sing to one another, reminding each other of what God has done for them in Christ, and so building each other up. But also, in our hearts, this singing is addressed to the Lord Jesus Christ, in thanksgiving.

Next we see that true spirituality is a spirituality of gratitude. Gratitude has, justifiably, been called the "heartbeat of Pauline spirituality".[10] Indeed, there are few activities which mark the spiritual person as distinct from the unspiritual more than thankfulness. One of the identifying marks of the ungodly is that they do not honour God as God *or give him thanks* (Rom 1:21). By contrast, in the words of St Augustine, the believer is a hallelujah from head to foot. Few prayers better express the breadth of the believer's thankfulness than the General Thanksgiving of the Anglican Prayer Book:

> Almighty God, Father of all mercies,
> We your unworthy servants give humble and hearty
> thanks for all your goodness and loving kindness to
> us and to all men.
> We bless you for our creation, preservation, and all

the blessings of this life.
But above all for your amazing love in the
redemption of the world by our Lord Jesus Christ;
For the means of grace, and for the hope of glory.
And, we pray, give us that due sense of all your
mercies that our hearts may be truly thankful and
that we may declare your praise, not only with our
lips but in our lives ...

Finally, as we've seen elsewhere in Paul's writings, being filled by the Spirit expresses itself in how people appropriately treat one another. Paul calls on Christians to submit to those who have authority over them.[11] The rest of the passage, through to 6:9, describes how this spirituality of submission expresses itself in the home, as Paul describes the spirituality of Spirit-filled husbands, wives, parents, children, masters and slaves. Again, this all serves to emphasize that biblical spirituality is not a spirituality for the recluse in his or her private cell. It is everyday spirituality, which is expressed in how a father loves and disciplines his children, and how a slave sincerely and enthusiastically serves his or her master. It is a spirituality which determines the kind of language that people use in talking to one another, how they spend their money, as well as how they sing when the church gathers together.

Spirituality and the word of God

Before we leave Paul, we need briefly to address two other aspects of Paul's 'spirituality'. Paul's description of the Spirit-filled life in Ephesians 5 shares a great deal in common with what he says in Colossians 3:16. There is the same emphasis on gratitude and singing. However, in Colossians, these activities are said to spring, not from the filling of the Spirit, but from the indwelling of the word of Christ. Paul writes,

> Let the word of Christ dwell in you richly,
> teaching and admonishing one another in all wisdom,
> singing psalms and hymns and spiritual songs, with
> thankfulness in your hearts to God (Col 3:16).

Of course, there is not an equivalence between the word of Christ, which is the gospel the believers received, and the Spirit of Christ. At the same time, there is clearly an intimate relationship between the two. To be filled with all the fullness of Christ cannot be separated from having the Spirit apply God's word to our lives. The songs we sing spring from what we know of God and his saving acts as recorded for us in the Bible. The thanks we render comes from our experience of God's goodness to us, which has come to us in the gospel of our Lord Jesus. Being richly indwelt by Christ's word, and being filled with his fullness, point to the same reality. In short, biblical spirituality is a spirituality of the word of Christ. It may be true that a person can have their mind filled with Christ's word and yet still be spiritually parched and fruitless. However, the converse does not apply: that one can grow spiritually apart from being deeply indwelt by the word of Christ. As the psalmist says,

> Blessed is the man who[se] ... delight is in the law of
> the LORD, and on his law he meditates day and night.
> He is like a tree planted by streams of water, that
> yields its fruit in its season, and its leaf does not wither.
> In all that he does, he prospers (Ps 1:1-3).

Spirituality and prayer

We have seen that contemporary spirituality is more concerned with the inner man, the health of the human soul or spirit, than the work of the Spirit of God in people's lives. While we have seen that biblical spirituality places its emphasis elsewhere, that does not mean that there is no concern in the writings of Paul for the inner being. In one of his finest examples of intercession, the apostle prays,

> I bow my knees before the Father, from whom every family in heaven and on earth is named, that according to the riches of his glory he may grant you to be strengthened with power through his Spirit in your inner being, so that Christ may dwell in your hearts through faith—that you, being rooted and grounded in love, may have strength to comprehend with all the saints what is the breadth and length and height and depth, and to know the love of Christ that surpasses knowledge, that you may be filled with all the fullness of God (Eph 3:15-19).

Essentially, there are two aspects of our humanity: the outer body which is wasting away, and the inner person which is being daily renewed. While the prayers of most Christians today seem to focus on the outer person (prayers for health etc), Paul's concern is the inner being. His prayer is that Christ may "dwell in your hearts through faith". "In your hearts" is no different from "in your inner being". It is that aspect of our humanity which controls our character, and prepares us for heaven. In the Bible, the heart is the centre of a person's personality, the thoughts, will, emotions, and whatever else lies at the centre of their being. When Paul prays for Christ to come and take up residence in our hearts, he is asking that he might be at the centre of our lives and exercise his rule over all that we are and do.[12] Of course, Christ already dwells in the heart of each believer, but the prayer here is that he might continue to do so, and more and more, cleaning out the junk rooms of our old self, and making for himself a home fit for a King.

The consequence of this indwelling is that the believer will be so established in love, that he or she will be able to comprehend even more wonderfully the extent of Christ's love for them. A knowledge of Christ's love for us is the soil in which spiritual growth blossoms, and it is the foundation on which a mature, Christlike personality is built. No matter how mature a Christian might be, there is still much, much more that he or she has to learn about the wonder of Christ's love for them. And this love is not something that we grasp only, or even primarily, on our own, in times of solitude and silence, but it is a knowledge that grows in our fellowship "with all the saints". As other Christians bring to us their insights into the word of God, or share their experiences of the love of Christ, our understanding of what Jesus has done for us grows, and our response of love and obedience is enhanced. Indeed, one can say that there is a relationship between the degree of our Christian maturity, and the extent to which we appreciate the love of Christ. Until God, by his power—and only by *his* power—increases our understanding of the extent of Jesus' love for us, shown centrally in his death and resurrection, then our Christian growth will be stunted. This is Paul's point when he says that the goal of our being strengthened by the Spirit is that we might "be filled with all the fullness of God".

This sort of prayer, both in its form, and in its goal, is vastly different from the sort of contemplative prayer that mystics encourage. There is no encouragement here to wordlessness, or the repetition of phrases. Here is word-full prayer. Not wordy, but prayer that feasts and feeds on the truths of what God has done for us in his Son. This love "surpasses knowledge", not in the sense that we have to submit ourselves to 'unknowing' in order that we might truly come to know, but rather that Christ's love is so great that we will never be able to sound its depths. No matter how much we grow in our knowledge of this love (and grow we must), there will always be so much more for us to explore and experience. God, out of the riches of his glory and strength, wants to empower his people to grow in this knowledge.

The spiritual person is a man or woman indwelt by God's Spirit, a person who is being transformed by that Spirit into the likeness of Jesus. Therefore, prayer "in the Spirit" (of which Ephesians 3 is a wonderful example) is prayer for people that this goal of transformation might come to fruition in their lives. It is prayer that they may be filled with all God's fullness, that they might be holy as he is holy, that they be finally found conformed to the image of the Son of God.

This has been a brief sketch of Paul's surprising picture of life in the Spirit. It is, in a word, the life of godliness. It is a life rooted and grounded in God's love for his people, expressed in all that he has done for us in Jesus. It is a life that responds to this love with heartfelt thanks and praise, and a commitment to love others with the kind of love that God has shown us. This life of godliness grows and matures in the crucible of suffering, and in the midst of a life marked by frustration. Yet, all the time, it is focussed on the Lord who reigns on high and for whom we live, day by day, in the eager expectation of beholding him face to face.

ENDNOTES

1 Peter is the only other New Testament author to employ the term 'spiritual' (1 Pet 2:5,6).

2 James DG Dunn, *The Theology of Paul the Apostle*, p. 76.

3 The meaning of this verse has been hotly debated. Some commentators, like Douglas Moo, argue that "the righteous requirement of the law" is the demand for perfection, which was fulfilled by Christ, and since we are incorporated into him, therefore in us (*The Epistle to the Romans*, Eerdmans, Grand Rapids, 1996, pp. 481ff). Glenn Davies argues that it is the penalty for sin, which Christ took upon himself on the cross (*Faith and Obedience in Romans*, PhD Thesis, 1987, pp. 177-178). David Peterson argues that it refers to both Christ's work in perfectly fulfilling the law's demands, and the empowering of the Spirit which enables us to a new obedience to these demands (*Possessed by God: A New Testament Theology of Sanctification and Holiness*, Apollos, Leicester, 1995, p. 170). For a fuller defense of the position I am presenting here see Gordon Fee, *God's Empowering Presence: The Holy Spirit in the Letters of Paul*, Hendricksen, Peabody, 1994, pp. 534-538.

4 Fee, *God's Empowering Presence*, p. 563.

5 Moo, *Romans*, p. 502.

6 Joel recounts his experience of captivity in Joel DeHart, *The Upper Hand: God's Sovereignty in Afghan Captivity*, Islamabad, 1994.

7 Demarest, *Satisfy Your Soul*, p. 285.

8 Bilquis Sheikh, *I Dared to Call Him Father*, Word, Waco, 1980, p. 52.

9 Peter T O'Brien, *The Letter to the Ephesians*, Eerdmans, Grand Rapids, 1999, p. 392.

10 RP Meye, 'Spirituality' in Gerald F Hawthorne, Ralph P Martin and Daniel G Reid (eds), *Dictionary of Paul and his Letters*, IVP, Downers Grove, 1993, p. 915.

11 It is hotly debated whether by this term 'submission', Paul implies a mutuality of relationships in which there is no subordination, or whether the term refers to submission to those who, in some way, hold a superior rank. For a persuasive defense of the latter position see O'Brien, *Ephesians*, pp. 399-404.

12 O'Brien, *Ephesians*, p. 259.

Chapter 9

Thirsty Evangelicals

IS THE GRASS greener on the other side of the spiritual hill? The testimony of many who have left the evangelical field for mystical meadows or pentecostal pastures is that the grass over there is sweeter and more satisfying. This is what makes books which commend the mystical way so appealing to Christians. Who doesn't want a deeper and more satisfying relationship with God in their inner being? Who doesn't want, in Demarest's words, "to know His presence and to sense His work in my life"?

As I have spoken to Christians about the spirituality phenomenon in our society, it is at this point that their interest level peaks. Hearing about various alternative spiritualities arouses mild interest, but as soon as one speaks of the longing of Christians for a deeper encounter with the Lord, and the dissatisfaction that many feel with their own personal relationship with God, then it becomes clear that the discussion has left the realm of the academic. Immediately we are discussing a question of vital concern to many.

The most striking aspect of so much of contemporary evangelical spirituality is that it is essentially a cry of the heart. In its various forms it is an expression of the hunger and thirst that gnaws at the heart of every converted man or woman for a deeper experience of God, and a meaningful relationship with him and other people. Not surprisingly, then, there is a great temptation for hungry and thirsty evangelicals to explore and see if other traditions really can supply the 'something more' that their hearts tell them must be there in a relationship with Jesus Christ.

We have argued that this desire for a deep and eternally satisfying relationship with God, and an experience of daily fellowship with him, is entirely natural for those renewed and indwelt by the Spirit of God. One of the frustrations of life outside of Eden is that all people, Christian and non-Christian, must groan under the curse of living in a world from which God has hidden his face. Even we who have met God in the Lord Jesus, who comes to us by his Spirit, revealed in his Word, still long to see him face to face. So this, in part, explains why people might search for 'something more', even if the price they have to pay is a degree of theological compromise.

However, this only partially explains why an increasing number of people seem to be making an exodus from evangelicalism. A sense that the grass is greener over there also implies that there is something inadequate about the grass right here. Certainly, as I talk with evangelicals, and largely those who remain committed to the evangelical tradition, serious concerns are raised about the kind of piety or spirituality that is presented to them. I find again and again that these evangelicals feel a degree of sympathy for those who pursue other types of spirituality in the hope that they will draw them closer to the Saviour they love.

After an election, while the victors celebrate, the defeated party usually withdraws for a time of sober re-evaluation. A voting shift in the population towards one party means necessarily a shift away from another party. It would be foolish for a party to place the blame for its defeat wholly and solely on the shoulders of others. There may be some validity in blaming the electorate, or putting the defeat down to various social or economic factors, or the duplicitous campaigning of their opponents. The real issue the party must address is, if even some of the party faithful are deserting us, are there good reasons why?

The point of my comparison is, hopefully, obvious. It is

helpful to see the current spirituality phenomenon against the background of social changes over the last half century. These, indeed, explain to a large degree why so many people in our society are looking for these kinds of spiritual connections. Further, it is right to examine the phenomenon theologically, and understand that the attraction of the various spiritualities actually tells us more about the sinful human condition than the character of true spirituality. However, it would be one-eyed for evangelicals not to stop and ask themselves if there is something about their expression of evangelicalism which may be contributing to the sense of spiritual dryness that many people are testifying to. Is our expression of evangelicalism really as biblical as we think it is? Or have we adopted practices and attitudes, either by habit, or perhaps because of the impact of our own cultural background that, in fact, owe more to culture and tradition than they do to the Bible?

In other words, should we not address the fact that people's attraction to alternative spiritualities may also be an expression of some dissatisfaction with, and an implicit protest against, a particular brand of evangelical spirituality? In this last chapter I want to address some of the blind spots that we may have in the evangelicalism of which I am a part. This is reformed Anglican evangelicalism. To some extent, what I say here will have particular application to this brand of evangelicalism. Nevertheless, some of the issues will, I hope, have a wider relevance. Certainly, the movement of evangelicals away from traditional styles and practices of evangelical piety to others which, previously, would have been considered theologically suspect, is a global phenomenon. A few years ago, Wheaton College professor of New Testament Gary Burge wrote an article in *Christianity Today* entitled, 'Missing God at Church'.[1] Here he described the pilgrimage of an increasing number of conservative evangelicals away from mainstream evangelicalism into various forms of Christian mysticism. While admitting that he, himself, is still committed to evangelical orthodoxy, he, too, feels that "somewhere the mystery of God has been lost".

Of course, one should quite rightly respond that much of the 'mystery of God' was lost at the incarnation, when the unseen God made himself known. But if Burge means that the contemporary church has lost a sense of awe and fear in the presence of God, then such an observation is difficult to refute. Even more, if sermons and Christian conversations provide trite and simplistic answers to profound and often deeply unsettling questions, and leave no space for the mystery of God's providence, then we certainly want to stand against them. However, if Burge is calling us back into the cloud of unknowing, then to those who walk in the light this is a journey away from the knowledge of God which comes to us in the gospel of the Lord Jesus. Whatever is meant by this elusive statement, his comments testify to the fact that while the symptoms of the expression of evangelical thirst may have a particular and regional character to them, evangelicalism worldwide is facing similar problems.

In brief, the complaint most often raised against the form of evangelicalism presented to many in our churches is that it is too dry and cerebral. The message of the gospel is that God has come amongst us in his Son and that the Spirit of God still reveals the Son to us as his word is taught and proclaimed. The Bible is clear that Christians have a genuine relationship with the Lord of heaven and earth. We know and personally experience God in Christ through the ministry of the Holy Spirit. Yet, much of contemporary evangelicalism seems to have lost some of the personal and affective dimension of our relationship with the Saviour. This is evident in a number of areas.

1. Evangelical God-talk

How we articulate our faith, of course, reflects how we understand our faith. 'God talk' is not something we think much about because it is a way of speaking that we have grown up with. It is not until you listen to the way people of other cultures speak that you realize that the way you communicate and relate together is different. For example, the humour of Australians is quite unique. We ridicule and insult people we like. It's our way of showing affection and respect! It goes without saying, that foreigners find this a most peculiar way of expressing admiration. Indeed, it is not until one sees the hurt expression on the face of a friend whom you've just lovingly insulted, that you realize that this is a way of speaking that is culturally particular and, perhaps, not always godly.

We need, similarly, some perspective on how we talk about God and our faith in him. Have you ever wondered, for example, why we make more of *what we believe* than *whom we trust*? We are in love with the gospel, but feel a little uncomfortable with Jesus. Recently, I received a brochure which was commending the opportunities for country ministry in rural New South Wales. The attractively produced brochure began by commenting that a lot of **gospel-minded** men and women dismiss ministry in the bush. We were then told of the hard work in **gospel ministry**, and we were exhorted to promote the **gospel** in country NSW where there has been considerable **gospel growth**. The bishop of the area is known as a man who has promoted **the gospel**. It is at this point that the Lord Jesus makes his only brief, and rather tangential appearance in the script, when we are told that the Diocese wants Christ-like believers. However, the Lord won't appear again and it is back to the gospel. We are then informed about **gospel ministry** in the towns, and the strategy of fishing from a good boat (that is, Anglicanism) in order to tell others **the gospel**. The appeal is made for enthusiastic **gospel-minded** men and women so that this area may become a stepping stone to other **gospel fields**. Finally, those who respond to this call can be encouraged that the other clergy will help **gospel workers** to stick at it.

It is gospel, gospel, gospel, but where is Jesus? This is our God-talk, and from one point of view, it is appropriate language. The gospel referred to here is the gospel about Jesus, and you could say that this way of speaking is just a shorthand way of referring to the work of our great God and Saviour, the Lord Jesus Christ. However, when one reads the writings of the apostle Paul, for example, the great champion of this gospel, it is striking that he does not talk in this way. For example, in Ephesians 1 the apostle writes,

> Paul, an apostle of **Christ Jesus** ... Grace to you and peace from **God our Father and the Lord Jesus Christ**. Blessed be the **God and Father of our Lord Jesus Christ**, who has blessed us **in Christ** ... just as he chose us **in him** ... he predestined us for adoption **through Jesus Christ**.

Indeed, Paul will speak by name of the one he loves some fifteen times in these opening verses before he even mentions the gospel. The contrast with the way Paul verbalizes his faith and the way it is spoken about in many Christian circles is marked. Sometimes, evangelical Christians talk about their faith as if it is essentially a creed we subscribe to, rather than a person we belong to. When we speak of sharing our faith with someone it can sound more like we are trying to convince them to ascribe to a coherent theological world view, than introduce them to a Saviour who loves them and gave himself for them. Of course, it is not a case of either/or, but we should be aware of the dissonance between our God-talk and Paul's.

Related to this is our way of articulating the purpose of our life and ministry. When asked what they hope to do when they finish theological college, evangelical theological students will regularly describe their ministry in terms of 'teaching the Bible'. The goal of Christian ministry becomes the reading, studying and teaching of the Bible. This, however, runs into the danger of confusing the *goal and purpose* of our life and ministry, with the *means* by which we achieve the goal. We saw from the last chapter that the goal of our life is to grow in our knowledge of Christ, that we might be conformed to his image. The purpose of our ministry, in Paul's terms, is that we may all "attain to the unity of the faith and **the knowledge of the Son of God**, to mature manhood, **to the measure of the stature of the fullness of Christ"** (Eph 4:13).

I would hope that students come to theological college in order to grow in the knowledge of God and Christ. I hope that we are committed to being part of the church because we desire to meet with Christ in the presence of his people. Biblically, the great purpose of our lives is to glorify God. Yet, as you listen to Christians, and particularly those in paid Christian service, then you could easily get the impression that the chief end of man is 'to read the Bible and study it forever'. I do not want to diminish for a moment the importance of the word of God in the life of the believer. It is the means God has given to us for our coming to know him and grow in this personal knowledge. But the knowledge of God is our goal in life. The most basic means to achieve this end is the study of his word. We must be careful not to confuse the *goal* with the *means* God has given us to achieve this goal.

I suspect that for many of us there is a certain emotional security in talking about a set of propositions, and an accompanying emotional unease in talking about a waiting Father, a loving Saviour and an indwelling Spirit. Yet, the price we pay for consistently depersonalising our message is that our proclaiming of the gospel of the Lord Jesus can lose some of its force and appeal. More than that, in the presence of one another, we can disguise the fact that our coming together is to meet with a living Lord and Saviour.

The most popular evangelistic tool in recent years has undoubtedly been the *Alpha* programme, coming out of Holy Trinity Church in Brompton, and presented by Nicky Gumbel. Its success is due, in large part, to the fact that it has tapped into people's needs and desires for connection. It presents the gospel in the context of a meal and relationships. The course, rightly, has received criticism for some of its serious theological weaknesses, in particular its imbalanced emphasis on speaking in tongues, with the implication that it is the usual evidence of the filling of the Spirit. However, there is no denying the appeal of Nicky Gumbel as a communicator. One of the most striking features of his teaching, and one of its appeals, is that he consistently directs people to the person of Jesus Christ. He never speaks simply of the 'gospel', but always, "the gospel of the Lord

Jesus". This both makes it clear that there is only one piece of good news, that concerning Jesus Christ, but it also personalizes the message. We all believe that the greatest drawcard of Christianity is Jesus Christ. He is an astonishingly attractive and compelling personality. It is he that we present, both to believer and unbeliever. We need to re-examine our God talk, and ensure that both the content of our faith, and the verbal expression of that faith, rightly reflects the scriptures.

2. Christian experience

It follows that if our relationship with Jesus is personal it must also be experiential. It is increasingly uncommon for Christians today to speak of their faith in terms of 'having a relationship with Jesus Christ'. This is due, in part, to the facile and foolish ways in which such a relationship is often expressed in popular piety. For example, growing up as a Christian I used to sing, "He lives, he lives, Christ Jesus lives today. He walks with me and talks with me along life's narrow way". This makes the Lord Jesus sound like the neighbour next door that I go for an early morning stroll with each morning. There is enormous appeal in talking of our relationship with God in that way, but it really cannot survive careful theological scrutiny.[2]

When we talk about our relationship with God, we can give the impression that it is a relationship just like any other person-to-person relationship. But, of course, it is not. There are some very significant differences. While God is a person, his personhood is different from ours. For one thing, his personhood is uncreated; as a person he is without beginning or end. By contrast we are created persons. Further, God is one being in three persons. What is more, God is spirit. Human beings relate to each other through their bodies. We see, hear, and touch each other. God is the only unembodied person that we relate to. As Graham Cole points out, this is one of the major reasons most Christians find prayer so difficult. Our personal relationship with God is the only one we experience which isn't bodily.

What all this means is that we simply cannot relate to God in exactly the same way as we would to another human being. God has come to us in his Son and despite the chorus, this Son is not found to be walking with me along the road outside my home. This Son is reigning with his Father in heaven, and we wait in hope for his glorious appearing. It follows, then, that we must be careful how we speak about relating to this God; but relate to him, we do! For the Son comes to us in the person of the Spirit, who reveals Jesus to us, produces in us love for him, and the desire to communicate with him through prayer and reading his word. This is profoundly personal and experiential.

Let a Piper play a tune

The Christian's experience of God is one that fundamentally comes to us through the word of God. However, this ought not to be something dry, cerebral, and merely intellectual. It is the gospel which brings us into a relationship with God, and it is his word, which is bread from heaven, that continues to nourish us spiritually.

This is exemplified in an excerpt from the writings of John Piper, a writer who encapsulates the healthy holism of a genuine evangelical spirituality which is properly intellectual, deeply passionate, and consistently Christ-centred and other-person centred, while all the time rooted in the scriptures.

In a meditation in his book *A Godward Life*, entitled, 'Monday Morning Meditation on Thirst', Piper reflects on John 4:13-14:

> Everyone who drinks of this water will be thirsty again, but those who drink of the water that I will give them will never be thirsty forever. The water that I will give will become in him a spring of water welling up to eternal life.

Piper's comments on this verse are noteworthy for two reasons. Firstly, he acknowledges the reality of spiritual thirst. He speaks of his own thirst for God and the fact that "almost every believer who comes into my office thirsts". Yet his dilemma in this reflection is, how could believers continue to thirst when Jesus has said that once we have drunk of the life-giving water we will never thirst again?

However, also of interest are the terms in which Piper frames his resolution to this dilemma. He writes,

> The Lord answered. He showed me the rest of the verse and shed on it a light I had never seen before ... Jesus answered the only way I know him to answer. He opened my eyes to see the meaning of what he said in the Bible. I had rememorized the verse very early Sunday morning for my own soul and for possible use in the pastoral prayer. So as I prayed, the materials of divine communication were in place. As I cried out, the second half of the verse spoke. Jesus spoke. With it came an answer. Not an audible voice, but the voice of Jesus in the Word illumined and applied by the Holy Spirit.

Briefly, the answer is that while our thirst for God is quenched by the Spirit of Christ revealing himself to us in his word, this never obliterates the thirst, lest we lose our impulse to come to him again and again for all that God promises to be for us in Christ. However, Piper appropriately describes this realization as Jesus speaking to him and he hearing that voice. This is the voice of a divine-human relationship and one that is profoundly experiential. In other words, Piper is aware that in answer to his prayer, the Lord opened his mind to understand more profoundly the scripture before him. A man cries out to his God. God addresses him through his word. And this divine word brings understanding, comfort, and a firmer resolve to continue to return, again and again, to the water of life. It is an example of a vibrant evangelical faith or, if you like, spirituality, understood as life in the Spirit. It is listening to the voice of God in Christ, as it is mediated to us by the Holy Spirit in the word, which draws us back to Jesus that he might deepen our fellowship with him, so that we might be his people in the world.

Ordinary and extraordinary experiences of God

In one of his short stories, 'A Fragment about Living', Geoffrey Bingham recounts an experience of God which he had when a POW in Changi prison camp, during World War II. He had a badly injured leg, and physically he was very weak. On this particular day, while hobbling inside the camp, he felt so weak that he "wanted to slip towards the earth … and finally give way to sleep and the grey blank that was forming in his mind". It was then, Bingham recalls, that he heard "the Voice". This is how he recollects the event:

In fact he knew it was the Voice. It said strongly and clearly, and in Elizabethan English, "Thou shalt not die, but live, and declare the works of the Lord". The strong voice was patient, but it was firm. A thrill ran through him. Suddenly he realized the voice was not in his head, nor even in his heart, but outside of him. It had come through the atmosphere of the tropical island. It had located itself in a prison camp. It was speaking directly to him.

He knew then that, from this point, there would be no senseless fear, no wasted emotion of terror. He knew the machine-gun nests of guards. He knew the vulnerability of each prisoner. He knew his own weakness. But then *he knew he was not going to die!* Not anyway until he had declared the works of the Lord.[3]

When he returned to his room, Bingham searched his Bible to see if he could locate the words he had heard. He finally found them in Psalm 118:17. In a situation of extreme suffering and hardship, God in his mercy had, in a special and unusual way, brought to his servant a word of comfort.

What are we to make of experiences of God like this? We do need to affirm the unusual character of such an experience. Experience of God is not always so extraordinary. In a society hungry for tangible, spectacular experiences of God, Christians can easily be tempted to minimize or denigrate the very many, daily experiences we have of the grace and goodness of God. There is something tragic in hearing a Christian say things like, "I haven't seen an answer to prayer in ages", or "I can't remember the last time I experienced God". Constantly I pray, "give me today my daily bread", and for as long back as I can remember the Lord has faithfully and, indeed, abundantly answered that prayer. Each day he amazingly sends rain to water the earth, he causes the sun to rise, and he grants health and strength to our bodies. It is only because they happen so regularly that we cease to think of these experiences of God and his grace as spectacular.

In fact, so consistently do we experience such blessings from God that we can become blasé about them. Many modern films have remarkable special effects. In the past couple of years I've seen the Titanic sink, a tidal wave destroy a city, and the attack on Pearl Harbour—each one spectacularly realistic. Indeed, I've now seen so many special effects in so many films, that it is hard to really impress me any more. What once made us breathless as we sat in the cinema is now commonplace. We can feel this way about the amazing works of God which he daily performs before us. If the rising and setting of the sun no longer fills you with wonder, you're going to be pretty hard to impress!

So, the first thing we need to do is to recapture the wonder of God's daily works of grace and power. But, what about these more unusual, or perhaps less common, works of God to which Christians from time to time testify? In short, that the living God should do this sort of thing should neither surprise us nor alarm us. Yet, remarkably, it appears to both surprise and alarm some evangelicals. Much of the character of contemporary evangelical piety appears to be a reaction and, indeed, an over-reaction, to the excesses of charismatic Christianity. Some people from that tradition feast on stories of miracles as their daily spiritual diet. Some of these stories may be true, many appear spurious. More serious still, God is said to communicate to his people through personal experiences and words of knowledge, while the inspired Word of God is marginalized as the source of divine communication. Surrounded on every side by an infatuation with the spectacular, the supernatural, and the subjective, evangelicals have emphasized the objective nature of our faith, and the fact that God usually works in our world in ordinary means. However, an unfortunate consequence of evangelicals' appropriate criticism of this uncritical infatuation with the miraculous, has been that anything which smacks of the subjective or the out-of-the-ordinary is now seen as suspect and the 'thin edge of the wedge'.

How, though, should we think theologically about the more unusual experiences of God to which some Christians bear witness? Following traditional Reformed theology, Graham Cole gives us a helpful way forward.[4] He points out that there are two kinds of blessings that God gives to his people. Firstly, there are those things which, in his word, he has promised to do for us. For example, he has promised to hear our prayers, to forgive our sins, and not to put us through a temptation for which there is not the grace and strength to persevere. These are *God's covenanted blessings*. We can, rightly, expect such blessings, and encourage other believers to look for them and expect them as well. These are blessings that each and every believer, on the basis of the promises of God, can expect to see and experience in his or her life.

However, there are also blessings which we have no warrant biblically to expect, which nevertheless the Lord might graciously give to some people. These would include things like a long, pain-free life, or wealth, or hearing the voice of God. These are *God's uncovenanted blessings*. There is no promise in the Bible that in times of stress or difficulty you will hear the voice of God. There is no guarantee that, like Daniel, you will be wonderfully delivered from the jaws of a pack of hungry lions. However, there is a promise that in such troubling times his word will be a light to your path. There is the assurance that when you walk through the valley of the shadow of death, God will be with you. Therefore, in times of particular hardship we ought to read his word more diligently so that we can respond to the crisis in a God-honouring way. However, should God in his mercy grant to one of his children a special word of comfort, as he did to Geoffrey Bingham in that prison camp, then this blessing is to be received with joy and thanksgiving.

The common mistake which Christians make when such experiences come is to theologize about them in an unbiblical and unhelpful way. This is done when such experiences are spoken of as if they are normative. Other Christians then begin to wonder if they are missing out, or are second-class, because God hasn't spoken to them. It is a short step to then make such experiences prescriptive. So, books are written providing techniques for getting experiences, or explaining why every Christian ought to expect them in his or her life. Finally, such experiences become the subject of our proclamation. All such steps are theologically unwarranted and pastorally unhelpful.

Christians ought not to be unnecessarily alarmed or disturbed when they hear reports by other believers who have had experiences of God in terms of visions, dreams, the voice of God, ecstatic experiences of prayer (such as, for example, may accompany times of revival). God is gracious and, while he has not promised such experiences, he may in his mercy give them. The other trap that people easily fall into, though, is to be too credulous or naive about such accounts. We need to continue to be discerning about claims to Christian experience. It is significant that Bingham's experience was of a word of scripture that came to him in a special way. Whatever genuine experience a believer has will conform to the inspired revelation God has given to us in his word.

At the same time, we need to recapture the wonder of the everyday experiences of the mercy of God. Why should the sudden removal by God of a serious illness (which might cut short my life) in answer to prayer, be more wonderful and praiseworthy than the provision of fried chicken and vegetables (which prolongs my life), also given by the same Lord in answer to prayer? Perhaps, if the gift of our daily bread were not to come to us so often, and so generously (as is the life situation of many Christian believers), then we (like they) would see such provisions for the wonderful experiences of God that they really are!

Related to all of this is our increasing suspicion of the place of the testimony. Testimonies which for so long have been a staple of evangelical piety now have become suspect and superfluous. "Other Christians go on about what God is doing in their lives, but we tell people what God has done for them in Jesus Christ!" Of course, the gospel is about what God has done for us in Jesus, and this should always be our focus. We need to guard against the danger of presenting a gospel message which is more about the life stories of men and women, than the God who made them and redeemed them. Nevertheless, this God is the living God, and still draws people to himself. He still answers prayers. He still works in his people's lives in wonderful ways to achieve his good purposes for them. In hearing God-centred testimonies of the ongoing work of the living God in applying the gospel to the lives of his people there is great encouragement. Frankly, I find it hard enough as it is to live by faith and not by sight, without the struggle being made more difficult by the banishment from our gatherings and conversations of reports of the triumphs of the gospel, or the gracious providential work of the Heavenly Father in bringing his many sons and daughters to glory.

I recently heard a young Chinese couple speaking, in faltering English, about coming to faith in Christ out of a background of atheistic communism. The interviewer asked the young man, what difference knowing Christ had made in his life? He replied, with courageous honesty, that before he had met the Lord Jesus Christ he had hated Japanese people, but now, because of what Jesus had done and taught, he knew that he could no longer hate them, and that he had come to love them. To hear this young believer with transparent candidness share how the living God had so profoundly changed some deeply ingrained attitudes and emotions was very moving and encouraging.

We saw in the opening chapter that many of the spiritualities out there in the marketplace come replete with testimonies of how marvellous this or that life-transforming therapy has proven to be. On the one hand, the effect of all this might simply be that the relativistic nature of such spiritualities is reinforced: "what works for you is fine; but it doesn't work for me". On the other hand, it also indicates that people tend to grant a degree of authenticity to those 'spiritual connections' that are seen to be real and make a difference to one's life. The fact of the gospel is that it is—and only the gospel is—the power of God for salvation. God's gospel, by the power of his Spirit, transforms people's lives in truly dynamic ways. It changes attitudes, lifestyles, relationships, behaviours. Hatreds give way to love. Self-centredness is transformed into other-person centredness. Hedonists practise self-denial. Liars tell the truth. The immoral pursue chastity. The proud long to be humble. Only the gospel of Jesus Christ works such dramatic changes because, of course, such mighty works can only be achieved by God himself. As we preach Jesus Christ, we ought also to testify to the profound life-changes that an encounter with him inevitably brings.

3. Emotions and the Christian

What do the following have in common: dinosaurs, dodos, Tasmanian devils, and emotional Anglicans? You guessed it, they are all extinct species! Well, that may be a cheap shot, but there is an undeniable stoicism to how a good many evangelical Anglicans express their love and devotion to the Lord Jesus. I mention Anglicans because that's the species that I have the most to do with. However, my suspicion is that a fair degree of stoicism is to be found in the attitudes of evangelicals from a variety of traditions.

With respect to our emotions, I have often heard Christians admit, "We're frightened of them". Indeed, the perceptive, and slightly humorous comments of Robert C. Roberts may well reflect the attitudes of quite a few evangelical Christians:

> Aren't emotions, as such, pretty disreputable little items in the panoply of humanalia? Aren't they more like warts than like hands and fingers and toes, at best useless and at worst troublesome little accretions to the personality? Certainly, when we describe someone

as "an emotional type" we don't intend the epithet as a compliment. We mean that he is not quite in possession of himself. He is weak, immature, hollow, shallow, flabby, not 'together'. He cries easily, even on occasions which only by a stretch of the melodramatic imagination might be thought possibly to warrant a tear. He is useless in times of crisis, being discombobulated by circumstances which a more firmly drawn personality takes in stride.[5]

I've quoted Roberts at length, not just because I couldn't resist the temptation to include the word discombobulate in my book (I've looked it up, and it means, 'disconcert') but, more importantly, because he colourfully puts his finger on some of the unease we have about emotions. We are wary of emotional people, and emotionalism. However, as Roberts points out, emotional people are not weak because they have, or display, emotions, but because they display them inappropriately. Their feelings are often erratic, or they feel strongly about the wrong things, or the depth of their emotional display is not co-ordinate with that which has prompted it. Emotionalism is the deliberate manufacturing of an emotional response, such that it bypasses the mind and clear thinking on a matter. It is manipulative.

However, if we are concerned at the inappropriate emotionalism, or emotional manipulation that characterizes some expressions of Christian devotion, why aren't we equally disturbed by the emotional barrenness of some others? The accusation that evangelicals are "dry, intellectual, and cerebral" in the expression of their faith is an extremely serious one and, if true, (or, even if it contains a measure of truth), should cause us as much concern as any criticism of emotional manipulation.

A Christian faith of strong emotions that does not spring out of right and true thoughts about God is fundamentally flawed, and ultimately dishonours the God it purports to worship. Conversely though, a faith that understands and believes the great saving truths as they are revealed to us in the Bible, and then does not feel and express the personal impact of these truths in one's life, also must fail to properly render God the praise and honour that is his due.

The great 18th century theologian, Jonathan Edwards, in his classic work, *The Religious Affections*, argues that the soul is endued with two faculties. The first is the understanding, by which it is able to perceive, speculate upon and, finally, judge the truth or rightness of a matter. The other faculty "is that by which the soul does not merely perceive and view things, but is in some way inclined with respect to the things it views or considers". This part of the soul is variously called the inclination, or the will, or the heart. For Edwards, true religion consists not just in the understanding, but "in a great measure in vigorous and lively actings of the inclination and will of the soul, or the fervent exercises of the heart".

Edwards goes on to argue that God glorifies himself in his people by revealing himself both to their understanding and to their hearts. In other words, God is glorified in us, not just by our seeing and perceiving his goodness and greatness, but also by our then responding to what we have seen with joy and delight. Indeed, when people see God's glory and delight in it, God is actually more glorified than if they only see it, because his glory is then received by the whole soul, that is by both the understanding and by the heart.

I'm not saying bring back the choir, but ...

One of the anomalies of some expressions of modern evangelicalism is, what can only be described as, an ambivalence towards music and singing. Once again, this is in part a reaction to the over-emphasis on, and poor theologising about, music in so many churches today. The sheer banality of many contemporary choruses, and the constant repetition of these choruses during church meetings, together with the dumbing down of the term 'worship' such that it has now become synonymous with singing a particular kind of spiritual song, has prompted a much-needed response and critique from biblically-informed Christians.

However, another effect of this reaction is that evangelicals have unwittingly surrendered again (as they have in other areas, such as experience) much of the middle ground. Evangelicalism, once the spiritual wellspring from which our greatest hymns and songs flowed, has not only failed to produce many great modern Christian songs (although, thankfully, this has begun to change), but appears to have lost much of the joy of singing itself. While rightly arguing that the words of a song are of primary importance, and that in singing to one another we are involved in a form of teaching, the singing is often undertaken with all the joy and passion of the sermon (more of sermons, in a moment). As John Piper points out, song is neither prose nor poetry.

> The reason we sing is because there are depths and heights and intensities and kinds of emotion that will not be satisfactorily expressed by mere prosaic forms, or even poetic readings. There are realities that demand to break out of prose into poetry and some demand that poetry be stretched into song.[6]

We sing, not just because we are commanded to, or indeed, because it is something that people filled with the Holy Spirit are instinctively prompted to do (Eph 5:18-20), but because, as Piper wisely comments,

> the realities of God and Christ, creation and salvation, heaven and hell are so great that when they are known truly and felt duly, they demand more than discussion and analysis and description; they demand poetry and song and music. Singing is the Christian's way of saying: God is so great that thinking will not suffice, there must be deep feeling; and talking will not suffice, there must be singing".

I remember being at a Christian conference and, as was the custom, before the Bible study there was a lengthy time of singing. It didn't take long for the hands to be waving and the bodies swaying. Expressions on the faces were intense. Here were people expressing publicly their evident and genuine love for the Lord Jesus. But as I detached myself for a moment from the whole event, I asked myself why I felt uneasy and, indeed, even a little critical of what I was observing. I then looked at the songs we were singing. We'd sung four or five, all very short, and each one indistinguishable in its content from the one before. None of the songs had recounted much, if anything, of what the Lord had done for us in Jesus Christ. Indeed, the sum total of what we'd sung to each other in 15 or 20 minutes amounted to very little. Had you asked me later what we had sung about that morning I'm sure I couldn't have told you. I've no objection to singing with conviction, intensity and passion, but at least sing with such intensity songs that warrant it! These rather vacuous choruses, frankly, didn't deserve the level of response that was being given. Wherever the emotions were coming from, it was hard to imagine that it was the words of the songs that provoked them. This runs the risk of becoming emotionalism.

But what of much of the singing in many evangelical churches? Isn't the problem here the opposite one? We have at our fingertips some of the most marvellous Christian songs ever written. And there are being composed today new songs that rival the old classics in the beauty of their melodies, and the wonder and glory of their lyrics. We sing to one another the most sublime and thrilling truths imaginable. Yet, so often, we do so with little fervour or evident intellectual or emotional engagement. Which kind of singing is the greater travesty?

How can we explain the clear lack of enthusiasm for singing in so many evangelical gatherings? It is a thorough-going anomaly. The singing is often led by wooden leaders who seem to fear the reprimand of theological watchdogs who may interpret their smiles and joyful gestures as the first step on a slippery slide down into the murky depths of charismania. Equally inhibited, the congregations rarely sound like people who have been so gripped by the gospel which has changed their lives, that heartfelt, Spirit-inspired, God-centred singing is something they delight to participate in. We've all heard the quip by Christians that an eternity spent singing songs sounds more like purgatory than heaven. This says more about the quality of singing in our gatherings than the joy and hope of glory! I suspect that we will sing in heaven, because our first response on beholding the glory of God will not be to break up into discussion groups, but to break out into adoration and praise.

Singing intensifies our emotions and evangelicals need to

hear that this is a good thing. Of course, it can be manipulated and abused, as can every other dimension of a fallen personality, but we need to recognize that God has made us emotional beings, and we are to focus our emotions on the one who supremely deserves to be the object of our love, joy, fear, and praise.

The Delight of the Word

Of course, singing is only one expression of our delight in the glory of God. Hearing the word of God read and preached ought to be an experience which engages the whole personality. It is tragic to hear sermons on, say, the seriousness of sin, the majesty of Jesus, the assurance of salvation, the expectation of glory, delivered with all the passion one might show in giving street directions to a passing motorist. I well remember hearing a sermon on "the height, depth, length and breadth of God's love for us in Christ" (Eph 3:18) delivered throughout without a flicker of emotion. I daresay that had the preacher played mood music in the background, or had a choir softly humming a tune while he preached, then he would have been sternly chastised for cheap emotional manipulation. And rightly so. But is it any less a demeaning of the greatness and glory of the gospel to speak of such sublime truths as if one is describing the dimensions of a proposed extension to the house, and not the immeasurable limits of the divine love (indeed, I wonder if the former may have prompted more passion on the part of the preacher). What has happened to our evangelical piety when we allow such preaching to continue without challenge from the pulpits of our churches?

It would seem to most casual observers that there could hardly be a less emotionally engaging and more intellectually demanding activity than the writing of a detailed commentary on a book of the Bible. It requires careful (even laborious), painstaking analysis and research. Gordon Fee is the author of a massive (880 pages) and widely respected commentary on 1 Corinthians. Reflecting on the whole activity of commentary writing, Fee later recalled (and I happily quote at length):

> Finally, I must mention the several times when I had very personal encounters with the living God through the power of the text itself ... Perhaps for me the single most significant of these moments came at 13:4. One must first appreciate the kind of dread with which I finally came to these verses (13:4-7). Here is a passage so well known, and so full of inherent power, that comment by me would seem to be both profane and pedestrian. But as I began to reflect on the significance of the first two words on the list (longsuffering [KJV] and kindness), I was suddenly struck by the clear reality that these are two words that Paul elsewhere uses to describe the character of God (the passive and active sides of God's love). As I sat and reflected on what that meant, I was overwhelmed with an indescribable emotion, as it came to me that not only is God like this—eternally and faithfully so—but where would I be, and those I love, if it were not so. What if God loved with the same degree of longsuffering as I have towards those who have sinned against, or disappointed, me. It was one of those grand moments of hearing the gospel afresh and being renewed in the presence of God. It is also the kind of moment very difficult to capture in a commentary.[7]

Imagine that in writing a commentary! But the truth is, should we be able to imagine meditating upon the word of God and *not* experiencing such moments of profound emotion? The apostle Paul had such 'moments' as he wrote his letters. Reminding his readers of the greatness of God, he would burst out in doxology, heartfelt outpourings of praise to God. Rightly understood, the gospel will be deeply felt. This is a hallmark of evangelical piety, and while continuing to eschew false expressions of emotionalism, which are contrived, we ought to recognize that the gospel of Jesus Christ will evoke a response of love and gratitude from the whole person, their heart, soul, and mind.

Personalities differ. Some people are just more naturally inhibited in how they express their feelings than others. Cultures differ. The expressions of grief or happiness vary widely from people to people. What I have written is not a call for uniformity in emotional expression. Nevertheless, too many evangelicals have taken shelter under the canopies of personality and culture and, in so doing, have justified a degree of stoicism which may be appropriate for adherents of pagan philosophies, but is quite inappropriate for those who have encountered the living God in the person of his crucified and risen Son. We are emotional beings and we need to recognize that we, in part, may be contributing to the exodus from evangelicalism by offering people an unbalanced way of responding to the gospel. More seriously still, we may in fact be failing to properly honour and praise our God who has created us to sing and make melody to the Lord in our hearts (Eph 5:19).

The first and great commandment is to love the Lord our God with all our heart, mind, soul, and strength. In other words, our response to the Lord is to be a fully human response. It is the appropriate response of the creature to the Creator. The call here is not a call to a new kind of mystical encounter with the Lord; one which elevates or isolates from the rest of our personhood the emotional or the experiential. Yet, at the same time it is a call not to be less than human in our daily expression of life in the Spirit.

ENDNOTES

1   *Christianity Today*, October 6th, 1997.

2   For some of the observations on the place of experience in the Christian life I am indebted to the excellent article by Graham Cole, 'Experiencing the Lord: rhetoric and reality', in BG Webb (ed.), *Spirit of the Living God*, Lancer, Sydney, 1992, pp. 49-70.

3   Geoffrey C Bingham, 'A fragment about living', in *Angel Wings*, New Creation Publications, Blackwood, 1981, p. 2.

4   Graeme Cole, 'Experiencing the Lord', pp. 60-61.

5   Robert C Roberts, *Spirituality and Human Emotion*, Eerdmans, Grand Rapids, 1982, p. 14.

6   John Piper, 'Singing and making melody to the Lord' (Ephesians 5:17-20). A sermon preached at Bethlehem Baptist Church, 28th December, 1997.

7   Gordon Fee, 'Reflections on commentary writing', in *Listening to the Spirit in the Text*, Eerdmans, Grand Rapids, 2000, pp. 22-23.

A Final Word

THERE'S EVERY REASON to believe that in our society spirituality will become an increasingly talked about and practised phenomenon. There is so much about it that appeals to Australians today. The new spirituality taps into the optimism that is evident in some parts of society. Enormous progress in science and medicine holds out great hope for the cure of various illnesses and, therefore, an even longer life. Some optimistic scientists are even forecasting that every disease will be able to be cured within this century.

Along with this the new spirituality holds out the promise of a richer and healthier spiritual life. Then, as we better understand ourselves and connect with others who have experienced the same enlightenment, together, with one spirit, we can tackle the problems that threaten to destroy the cosmos.

This is the gospel of the new spirituality: a relationship with the Other that pervades all reality. An experience of ultimate reality that will not accuse or condemn you, but will allow you the freedom to explore your own inner self in whatever way best enriches you. This is the context in which Christians proclaim an unchanging gospel. It is the gospel of a living Lord and Saviour. This God is personal and will encounter people in a genuine and meaningful way, although always and only on his terms, which are repentance and faith in his Son.

I remember a few years ago being in Lahore, Pakistan for

a conference. It was stifling hot, and the large church where we held the meetings only had tap water. With Pakistani tap water you often get more than you pay for! The Pakistanis attending the conference could drink the local water, since their cast-iron stomachs were largely immune to all the 'extra ingredients'. However, I knew that if I drank that water I'd be suffering the consequences for weeks. Still, nothing to fear, because all around me were billboards reminding me that *Coke* was the thirst quencher, that it "adds life" and it's "the real thing". There were plenty of shops with bottles of Coke in large freezers. I went to a shop, paid my equivalent of 15 cents, rolled the cold bottle over my forehead, and let the ice-cool Coke pour down my throat. It felt terrific. Yet, no sooner had I finished the drink, than my throat felt dry and parched again. I went back to that shop again and again. I must have wasted 75 cents that afternoon on *Cokes*! Later my American colleague turned up with a large cooler of cold, clean water. I can still recall the sensation. It was, quite simply, the best drink I've ever had.

Coke looks good and, for many, the taste is appealing, and if you're not really thirsty it can even be enjoyable. But as a genuine solution to thirst, it's useless. It's a fake. A false prophet. It can't deliver what it promises. I'm not surprised that in a world like ours it's the most popular drink on the market. We are a world full of people drinking Cokes on hot days, when there is a well of fresh, icy cold water right around the corner. People wander around Mind Body Spirit Festivals, or log onto bizarre websites, or go deep inside themselves to discover the spirit within, when just a prayer away, is the God and Father of Jesus Christ, their maker and redeemer.

It is our mission to expose the false superstitions of our

society, and confidently and winsomely present Jesus Christ, the bread and water of life. Our challenge is to proclaim this gospel and express this faith in a way that is faithful to scripture and meaningful to shoppers in the spiritual marketplaces all around us.

About Matthias Media

Matthias Media is an independent, evangelical, non-denominational company aiming to produce books and other resources of a uniformly high quality—both in their biblical faithfulness and in the quality of the writing and production.

For more information about our extensive range of Bible studies, books, evangelistic tools, training courses, periodicals and multimedia resources, visit us at **www.matthiasmedia.com.au** or contact us in any of the following ways:

Mail: Matthias Media
PO Box 225
Kingsford NSW 2032
Australia

Telephone: **1800 814 360** *(tollfree in Australia)*
9663 1478 *(in Sydney)*
+61-2-9663 1478 *(international)*

Facsimile: (02) 9663 3265 *(in Sydney)*
+61-2-9663 3265 *(international)*

Email: info@matthiasmedia.com.au